"In *Family Fundamentals*, m[barcode obscures text] handed us the tools to build [obscured] foundation for our family, but he has also entrusted to us a vision of redemption. The building blocks of Team, Time, Table, Tech, and Traditions are exactly what we need to build a family culture that will withstand the challenges of life. More importantly, he has given us a new vision of how to lay our family's foundation on the true Cornerstone, Jesus, and in so doing know how to be a picture of God's larger family to a hurting world around us."

—Noel Bouche,
Founder, Canyon Pathways

"*Family Fundamentals* is not only a written work but the lifelong example of Daniel's leadership when it comes to his family and what he hopes for all families. His passion to help families jumps off the pages with sound and practical advice for both everyday situations and long-term thinking. I highly recommend this book to all parents."

—Matt McKee,
Entrepreneur, Author of *Parenting in a
Tech World* and *Parent Chat*

"I am so excited about the content found within *Family Fundamentals*, and Daniel McKee is the perfect person to bring this content to life. Daniel is a master teacher who has honed the concepts in *Family Fundamentals* over the span of his successful ministerial career. In addition, I have personally watched as he incorporated the ideas found in this text in his own family. Is your family designed around individualism and a make-it-on-your-own mentality? The ideas and structure within

Family Fundamentals will radically change your approach and impact the influence your entire family has on God's Kingdom. I know because I have had the pleasure of testing some of these ideas within my own family. Enjoy!"

—Carl Swart,
Chief Operating Officer, ApprioHealth, Inc.

"I've known Daniel for years. He has always astounded me with his undeterred intentionality that bleeds out into every area of his life. He brings all of his joy and presence everywhere he goes. Whether he's preaching or playing soccer, Daniel is all in wherever he is."

—Mike Donehey,
Singer, songwriter, author of *Finding God's Life for My Will*

"As a career professional, this is a must read that really makes a difference with family. Daniel McKee has written an honest look at family life with action steps squarely grounded in our Father's teachings. It's made me a better leader for my family!"

—Han Oh,
Plant Manager, Shearer's Snacks

"Daniel has a great way of taking the dynamics of the modern family and giving them paradigms to create a new way of seeing individuals and the whole of the family. It's not just philosophical thoughts but real life tangible practices that any family can use."

—Alton Alexander,
Lead Pastor, Anthem House Church

"Daniel's practical framework for guiding and impacting families in an intentional Christ-centered way is amazing. This will benefit families of all stages."

—Matt Massey,
Lead Pastor, Vineyard Community Church

"The family has been under attack for generations. Unfortunately, too many people simply never knew or had the chance to live the foundations that create a strong and lasting family. In *Family Fundamentals*, Daniel McKee delivers actionable principles everyone can use to reconnect, set a clear vision, and create strategies that will build a legacy. Regardless of your personal history, *Family Fundamentals* helps you find grace to forgive the past and guidance to create an amazing future."

—Kelly Smith,
Partner and Lead Consultant, Thinkhaus Idea Factory

Healthy, Christ-centered families are one of the primary ways God intends to further the mission of His church. As I have watched Daniel McKee's ministry for well over a decade, I am convinced that the wisdom he offers in this book is something we need to hear.

—J. T. English
Lead Pastor, Story Line Fellowship, author of *Deep Discipleship*

FAMILY
FUNDAMENTALS

A Playbook for Family Legacy

DANIEL McKEE

Family Fundamentals
A Playbook for Family Legacy

Copyright © 2021 by Daniel McKee

Published by Lucid Books in Houston, TX
www.lucidbookspublishing.com

Scripture quotations marked (NIV) are taken from the Holy Bible, New International Version®, NIV®. Copyright ©1973, 1978, 1984, 2011 by Biblica, Inc.™ Used by permission of Zondervan. All rights reserved worldwide. www.zondervan.com The "NIV" and "New International Version" are trademarks registered in the United States Patent and Trademark Office by Biblica, Inc.™

Scripture quotations marked (ESV) are taken from the Holy Bible, English Standard Version®, ESV®. Copyright © 2001 by Crossway, a publishing ministry of Good News Publishers. All rights reserved. ESV Text Edition: 2016.

Scripture quotations marked (NLT) are taken from the Holy Bible, New Living Translation, Copyright © 1996, 2004, 2015 by Tyndale House Foundation. All rights reserved.

Scripture quotations marked (MSG) are taken from THE MESSAGE, Copyright © 1993, 2002, 2018 by Eugene H. Peterson. Used by permission of NavPress, represented by Tyndale House Publishers. All rights reserved.

ISBN: 978-1-63296-447-2
eISBN: 978-1-63296-449-6

Dedication

To my beautiful bride, Ashley; our children Caedmon, Chloe, Ansley, and Abram; and all future generations of Team McKee.

May you have courage to resist conforming to the pattern of this world as you are transformed by the wisdom of God. May you know and experience the joy of walking in His good, pleasing, and perfect will as you extend the McKee family mission. May the fire of God's presence in you continually bring light, warmth, and forever change.

CONTENTS

Preface

*F*IRST OF ALL, well done! You are investing time in and focus on one of the most important, enduring, and transformational aspects of life. Family is the most foundational building block for communities, churches, cultures, and civilizations. The health of any culture is directly tied to the health of its families. Since Western culture does not seem to be improving in either family or culture, this book is an attempt to cast new vision for modern families based on ancient, biblical wisdom.

Most people expect to be great parents or spouses because of their good intentions. They try to have a great family, but the challenges and complications of life war against their noble attempts. These obstacles, along with a confusing and chaotic culture, cause many family leaders to coast through family life in a sort of default mode. They deliver their best energy, strategy, and investment to their current jobs or hobbies, which often have a very limited legacy.

Many people hire personal trainers to help them succeed in fitness or business, but trainers for families are scarcely found. Yet we would say these relationships are significantly more valuable to us than our physique or finances. We usually only find therapists or counselors to help pick up the broken pieces of our struggling family journey that began with good intentions. But there is good news! The gap between the family God intended for us and the current experience of our homes can be brought closer by returning to the fundamentals and applying them as a family in regular practice.

Don't try to have a great family. Train for an enduring family legacy. This book, *Family Fundamentals*, is designed to ground you with a clear vision and strategy for your family and to build a legacy that will be honored long after your time on earth is done. By applying the principles set forth in this book, you will be equipped with tools to take practical steps forward and live with passion and clarity for your future family.

What is possible for your family? What image do you see of your family thriving? What imprint will your family leave on the community and world around you? Can you see it? Are you ready to start building toward that possibility?

It's never too late to invest in your family legacy. Even if mistakes have been made and relationships fractured and you pick this book up out of broken desperation, God is a redeemer. He will honor your efforts to work with Him, follow His way, and allow Him to heal your family. Even if your children are no longer in your home, you are still in a unique position to affect the enduring legacy of your family.

Your future family begins today by going back to the fundamentals of family.

The Power of Fundamentals

NFL teams tirelessly train and precisely prepare every year for a chance at the Vince Lombardi trophy. This trophy marks the crowning of the world championship football team—wait… isn't football only played in America? Anyway, the trophy is named after arguably the greatest coach in NFL history. As head coach of the Green Bay Packers, Lombardi never had a losing season and maintained a remarkable winning percentage of 72.8 percent (96–34–6) in regular season play and 90 percent (9–1) in the postseason, for an overall record of 105 wins, 35 losses, and 6 ties in the NFL. But Lombardi didn't start with a winning team in Green Bay. He stepped in after the worst season of Packer football history when the team finished with a record of 1–10–1.

Lombardi's first season was a significant turnaround to a winning record, and in his second season, the Packers went all the way to the Super Bowl, although they lost on the final play that stopped a couple yards short of the goal line. Lombardi vowed to his team, "This will never happen again. You will never lose another championship." Crazy enough, he was right. He never lost another postseason game. How did he deliver on this promise?

He focused wholeheartedly on the fundamentals.

At the beginning of training camp the following season, Coach Lombardi stood in front of a roomful of professional football players and held up a ball. He proclaimed, "This is a football." Then he proceeded to walk these professional athletes back through the foundations of every block, every tackle, and every step they would take on and off the football field. It felt painfully insulting at first, but returning to the basics reformed the entire way they performed. These fundamentals would guide them to their greatest highlights and deliver them from habitually negative cycles they had developed over time.

Lombardi emphasized the long-term consistency required: "Football is like life – it requires perseverance, self-denial, hard work, sacrifice, dedication and respect for authority."[1] Fundamentals are more concerned with the marathon ahead than the shortcut of today. Focused intensity over time develops momentum toward the end goal through habit formation. Habits develop outcomes more than intentions and desires. "Winning is a habit. Unfortunately, so is losing."[2]

Lombardi wasn't the only coach to return to the fundamentals to achieve success. John Wooden, the so-called Wizard of Westwood, led UCLA to 10 NCAA basketball titles in a 12-year period. Before his elite players stepped onto the floor of the court each season, Wooden walked them through how to put on their socks and tie their shoes. Tight shoelaces would help them avoid blisters, which would keep everyone on the floor for every practice and every game. He then coached each aspect of the game with absolute precision.

Steve Kerr took over the Golden State Warriors as a rookie coach in 2014 and led them to an NBA championship. He began training camp with basic passing and dribbling drills that frustrated the players. He believed if they could reduce turnovers and play more selfless basketball, they could win a championship, so he went back to the fundamentals. Selfless "small ball" not only transformed the Warriors but brought a wave of innovation to the entire NBA.

It works in sports, so what does that have to do with family? I'm glad you asked. What if your biggest issue in your family is not your current conflict but that you have forgotten the fundamentals? What if you keep having the same problems because you built your family life on broken foundations? What if your family could live together with passion and purpose to impact generations to come? These fundamentals are like roots of a tree. As we fortify the roots, we will be strengthened to stand through the chaos and confusion our family and our culture naturally offer. I'm so excited for your future family to experience the blessings of the basic foundations you will build or rebuild as you journey through the five fundamental T's of family—Team, Time, Table, Tech, and Traditions.

CHAPTER 1

Picture-Perfect Family

Desire

*B*EFORE WE JUMP into the fundamentals, it is important to understand our starting point. To better unpack the desires of our hearts and the reality of our families, let's begin with a common family experience.

It's family photo day! Who's excited? You're going to get the perfect picture of this stage of your family life. What do you envision? A beautiful fall day with colorful leaves? Walking the beach in matching outfits? Gathering around the fireplace in Pinterest-worthy layers and textures? It sounds so good, right? It usually ends up looking like a beautiful picture we are excited to share, but it's never quite as easy as it appears.

If you've ever tried to gather your family for a photo session, you know what it requires to get a perfect—or salvageable—photo. The process of getting everyone dressed is a small skirmish that usually gives ground to bribes and promises of treats if everyone can make it through the experience. To add insult to injury, the coordinated outfits somehow don't fit as well as you had hoped since the kids (and sometimes the adults) have grown since you picked them out.

As you drive to the beautiful scene, family attitudes are often the opposite of the setting. Some have the exact image in their mind of how they want it to look, and others want to be anywhere but there. As you scrunch together and act like you love each other, synchronous smiles and open eyes are tough to come by. Bribes and promises can often turn to threats and pleading as the dreamers of elsewhere require convincing. The original vision of lighthearted laughter together can turn to forced smiles and dried tears. Digital photography has helped this process greatly, but it's still difficult to capture the picture-perfect family moment we all dream of. Why is this such a common experience for families on photo day? Well, it's actually a really good metaphor for our entire experience as families.

We All Long for a Perfect Family

Built within everyone is a desire for a perfect family experience. Children want their parents to notice their achievements and affirm them with love and admiration. Parents hope for connection, closeness, and gratitude for their sacrificial serving. Siblings seek acceptance and companionship as they journey through life alongside a brother or sister. Grandparents long to experience gatherings of joyful celebration with generations around a table of honor, laughter, and love.

These desires are not wrong. They are actually really good and healthy desires. When present, these attributes of acceptance, affirmation, connection, gratitude, and celebration are a fountain of life. When they are absent, however, they are damaging to

2

development and relationships. When one family member feels they are not receiving their desired outcome, they often choose to withhold the desired outcome of another. These good desires twist into bad desires as we each have self-seeking visions for our family.

Many family problems can be understood in this twist. Each ideal vision from each person in the family is unique. The ideal vision of Mom is often drastically different than the ideal of Dad or a child. While one child wants to build a LEGO castle, another longs to creatively paint. Mom is seeing the potentially messy explosions, and Dad recognizes the long wavy grass that needs to be mowed. These competing visions are not necessarily negative, but they are often in contrast to each other. Or each time someone reaches for the remote control, it often results in a battle of selection and frustration.

We not only have competing desires around us, but we also have opposing desires within us. We long for more than we are currently experiencing but often can't name or isolate the source of our thirst. These echoes of Eden in our hearts call us back to the original ideal of family in oneness and unity.

In the first book of the Bible, God calls two people to create a singular unit. This oneness happens as two individuals leave their personal pursuits and become bound together physically, spiritually, and relationally. They are commanded to be fruitful and co-labor with God in the creative process. They are invited to walk with God and each other without comparison, shame, or competition. This freedom is short-lived as deceit and desire for independence invade the creation story. Unconditional love and oneness are traded for personal pursuit and isolation. This perfect experience is shattered, but a desire lingers in all of us for restoration and redemption of this original flourishing of oneness and unity in the family.

Reality

For family photo day, we often choose clothes we don't usually wear. We pose in ways we don't normally stand or sit together. There are distractions all around us that we have to manage—an annoying wind, moving backgrounds, bathroom breaks, sun in the eyes, or shadows on the faces. The moments we often hope to capture don't represent our normal life together.

What would be the most honest photo of your family? Everyone on a device in the same room in silence? An argument around the dinner table? In many families, members do their own thing separately, focused on different things, even in close proximity to each other. Many families also navigate the complicated reality of splitting weekends or sharing time due to divorce, relational struggles, or a spouse passing away.

Think about the competing dreams in your household. These dreams often turn into expectations of actions, attitudes, schedules, and everyone else's compliance. Healthy expectations can be beneficial, but often they function as a setup for regular disappointments. Have you ever been robbed of a good moment because you expected a better one? Do you overlook the things you could be grateful for and fixate on the few issues you overlooked or forgot? These are expectation issues more than situational ones. Yet from our expectations, disappointment grows in our hearts. Disappointment can easily grow into a bitter disillusionment with our current reality of marriage and family.

Individuals might begin looking around, wondering if it's better elsewhere, and run to other avenues of happiness and meaning. However, they can't quite shake the desire for a meaningful and life-giving experience of these core relationships we call family. This is a key realization...

There is always a gap between the ideal and the real.

The Ideal Family Is Not Real

Reality will never measure up to fantasy. You wanted healthy, obedient kids, and, well, that's not reality. You wanted a spouse who rubbed your back every night. Or maybe you dreamed of recreating the love stories in your favorite movies once a month...or year...or once. Or perhaps you hoped for a family reunion where everyone came together and made memories, but it's...complicated. Examples of this gap abound from the grand ideals of Christmas, vacations, and weddings to the more mundane aspects of cooking a new recipe, attempting to leave the house, or sleeping.

I've struggled with this imbalance between the ideal and the real when dealing with my own family. I have to choose to lay down some of the idealistic expectations I carry for my family and embrace what is in front of me. Why? It is difficult to find gratitude and joy in the realities of life because they can be so far from how I desire them to be.

In my own life, I needed to admit that I don't measure up to the ideals in my mind. I reluctantly admitted that I have wounded and will wound the hearts of my children, even if unintentionally. I have acted in unloving and selfish ways toward my spouse. And though I would love to say that's behind me, I'm human, so I

5

will undoubtedly act in selfish ways again that will not endear me to my wife. The results are what you might expect. Members of my family have reacted and will react against the pain I cause with painful responses of their own.

Prepared for these realities, I remain ready to apologize and offer forgiveness when needed. If I were clinging to my ideal family with all my entitlements as Dad, I would be constantly disappointed and demanding performance from everyone around me.

Pause for a moment, and ask yourself these questions:

- In what ways are my ideals driving disappointment with my family?
- How am I currently contributing to a less-than-ideal reality?
- What would it look like to start growing from where I am instead of where I want to be?
- How would others in my family describe their ideal?
- What would the first steps be toward a more ideal yet imperfect reality?

We have an ideal of connectedness and closeness that often doesn't match reality. We often expect to be great at family because we have children. Or we expect to have a great marriage because we exchanged vows. However, the only way to be great at anything is to learn and apply positive practices repeatedly. Then reality is transformed through this steady strengthening and repetition. The gap between the ideal family and the reality of our homes can be brought closer by returning to the fundamentals of family. But even with positive practices, we must remember...

Family Is Messy

Have you ever noticed that families or couples on TV never do laundry or clean the house? When we dream about the moments that make up our ideal family story, we often forget about the necessary, mundane tasks that are required to achieve our ideals. The ideal marriage for engaged couples never quite looks like the regular experience of seasoned spouses. Weddings and funerals bring out the messiness in every family. Children require so much cleaning up—from birth through potty training, meals, sleepovers, and graduation parties—and then they return with their own kids to continue bringing chaos into your attempts at order. And let's not forget the close and crazy distant relatives who know how to push all our buttons.

When we look down the family tree, we pretty quickly realize it's a mess, and we look at ourselves and think, yep, we're a mess too. Don't let the messy reality of your family become a total downer because it all points to a really important hope that anchors our lives.

In reality, you shouldn't be surprised to find challenges in your family. Competing dreams and visions in individual families and for the greater purpose of families exist in every culture, century, and civilization since creation. Even the families of the Bible are a mess. You would be hard pressed to find a significant family in Scripture after whom you would want to model your family. However, God's Word is filled with incredible wisdom and guidance. Where can we find hope?

Hope

Family is the source of our hopes and hurts, and the focus of most of our prayers. Why? Because there is an insatiable desire in all of us to be fully known and fully loved. We journey closely beside family in our most vulnerable, struggling, and painful moments as well as our greatest triumphs and celebrations. Family was designed by God to be a foundational source of identity and security. God made man in His image, and then He gave us the privilege to participate in making a child in our image as we pass on His truth and love to them.

We simply desire to love and be loved. If we're honest, however, the ideal for each of us is that we find love for ourselves in the good and hard times but only really need to be loving to others when it works for us. Family pries our selfish tendencies out of our daily experiences. Parenting shows us that our kids need something more than we can give. Marriage reveals that our spouse desires something more than even the best version of us. Our extended family often reflects a cornucopia of dysfunction while we long for the picture-perfect family.

Family Is a Perfect Picture of Our Need for God

Family delivers an overwhelming number of outcomes you can't control but maybe weren't meant to on your own. This is a good place of dependence and understanding of who God is and how He relates to us. The language of the Bible is often family language since God is presented as the Father and we are invited to live as His beloved kids. He invites you to come to Him to find healing for your soul and a source of love that doesn't run dry. The Apostle Paul tried to capture this when he wrote to the church in Ephesus in his less-than-ideal reality in prison.

Follow God's example, therefore, as dearly loved children and walk in the way of love, just as Christ loved us and gave himself up for us as a fragrant offering and sacrifice to God.

—Eph. 5:1-2

This language of family is at the heart of the gospel as we see Jesus's demonstration of love to allow us to be adopted into an eternal family. We are invited to live as dearly loved children because of what Jesus accomplished. What did Jesus do? He stepped in when the ideal was lacking. He stepped into our mess and loved despite the taunts. Despite the pain. Despite the naysayers and the temptations. He gave of Himself in the face of opposition in the form of healing, inviting ridicule to protect the defenseless, and ultimately giving His life for the good of others who were rejecting Him. He gave Himself up. He took the real punishment we deserved to offer restoration to the ideal for eternity to come. He offered unconditional love to those He fully knew with all their failures, inconsistencies, and triumphs.

This is how we know what love is: Jesus Christ laid down his life for us.

—1 John 3:16a

What love would cause someone to give themselves for the failures of others? How did Jesus walk this powerful but painful road? He lived and gave His life knowing the fundamental answer to facing opposition. Paul and many others who follow Jesus have learned this same secret to life and death. It comes down to two words...

Live Loved

Jesus knew He possessed the complete love of the Father, and no opinion or opposition could change His standing as God's beloved Son. He had love to give away. If we really believed we were already completely and constantly loved, it would change everything about our lives. Does any of this remind you of your role as a parent? Laying down your life for others? All of our fears, doubts, pride, guilt, and sin that entangle our hearts and minds can be traced back to a disbelief in God's unconditional and overwhelming love for us. Love has been demonstrated in its fullness in Christ and held out as a gift to receive. If we were living loved, we wouldn't be seeking to fill our tanks with the admiration of those around us; we would be looking to dispense this incredible love into their hearts. That is why our relationship with God is foundational to our lives—we must receive and know love in order to give love away.

And we ought to lay down our lives for our brothers and sisters.

—1 John 3:16b

Our desire to be loved often keeps us from being able to give love. The brokenness of life and our pursuits can keep us from knowing the security and experience of God's unconditional love for us. We have a tendency to chase people-pleasing and sources of identity in order to gain the attention and admiration of others. The prophet Isaiah speaks of these sources of love as broken cisterns that can't hold water. While we are thirsty, chasing love for ourselves, we often don't have much to give to those who are looking to receive it from us. When we embrace the love God has for us, we are running to an eternal source that doesn't run dry. He fills us to overflowing for the good of those around us, especially those closest to us in our families.

We love because he first loved us.

—1 John 4:19

If the goal is love and we all desire to be loved, what keeps us from experiencing this? There are several barriers in our hearts and lives that try to rob us of what God originally intended for us. Family reveals this emptiness in us as we continue to try to meet the needs of others but feel tired, overwhelmed, and inadequate. If you are trying to develop the perfect family on your own, it is a hopeless experiment. The expectations and disappointments that naturally rise will remind you repeatedly of your inability to control the outcome. In this less-than-perfect experience, we are invited to turn back to the Father to find His love, grace, and truth to guide us and fill us where we are lacking.

Two Truths That Transform Our Lives

- I am so desperate for help that Jesus had to die for me.
- I am so loved that Jesus was glad to die for me.

This book is not written by an author with a perfect family. My family has arguments, struggles, tears, wounds, doubts, and fears that mark our journey together. We are not the model to replicate, but our imperfections and regular wrestling have awakened us to something more important. We individually and collectively need Jesus to show us what love really is. When we embrace His love, we are enabled to extend His love through a generational legacy filled with hope and opportunity despite the challenges we face. We are also empowered to engage the broken reality of our family with gratitude for the blessings we experience.

However, be careful not to allow your family to become an idol in your heart. Family makes a terrible god. Our identities as sons and daughters of a heavenly and eternal Father signify the only perfect family experience. Our earthly families live with the goal of reflecting the eternal family through His presence working in and through our lives. The fundamentals are not a foolproof guide to a perfect family experience, but they will serve as anchors of clarity. It's surprising how profound simple truths are in a culture of chaos and confusion.

Now that we have broken the expectation of familial perfection and found the eternal source and satisfaction for our lives, let's build the fundamentals of family together.

As you process the love of God and His invitation to find life in Him, take time to reflect on Psalm 34.

I will extol the LORD at all times;
  his praise will always be on my lips.
I will glory in the LORD;
  let the afflicted hear and rejoice.
Glorify the LORD with me;
  let us exalt his name together.
I sought the LORD, and he answered me;
  he delivered me from all my fears.
Those who look to him are radiant;
  their faces are never covered with shame.
This poor man called, and the LORD heard him;
  he saved him out of all his troubles.
The angel of the LORD encamps around those who fear him,
  and he delivers them.
Taste and see that the LORD is good;
  blessed is the one who takes refuge in him.
Fear the LORD, you his holy people,
  for those who fear him lack nothing.
The lions may grow weak and hungry,
  but those who seek the LORD lack no good thing.
Come, my children, listen to me;
  I will teach you the fear of the LORD.
Whoever of you loves life
  and desires to see many good days,
keep your tongue from evil
  and your lips from telling lies.
Turn from evil and do good;
  seek peace and pursue it.

—Ps. 34:1-14

CHAPTER 2

Team

Definition

THE MOST IMPORTANT place to start building the fundamentals of family is with a clear definition of what family is. So my first challenge for you is to define the word and idea of *family*. Don't worry about writing the perfect definition or looking it up online. It is important to write the first thing that comes to your mind in order to understand your personal starting point. Use the white space below (or a sheet of paper or the notes on your phone if you don't like to write in books), and complete this sentence:

A family is...

Oh yeah, and don't skip this and just keep reading to find the answer. For those right-answer seekers, consider yourself busted.

It may sound like the simplest task, but as you begin to think through the broader experience of family in differing cultures and time periods, it may challenge your quick answer. Before

I write what I have come to see as a better and longer-lasting definition of family, let me share how I came to this conclusion.

Think of some of the moments in your life when everything changed. There are often milestones on our journey that shift the course of our lives. These moments are often dramatic at the time, but sometimes they are only recognized in hindsight after an unintentional direction shift. We don't see or feel the impact until later. Some of you may point to a tragedy, a person, a spiritual awakening, or key family moments such as getting married, having a child, or losing a loved one. There are many I could share from my journey, but one moment dramatically shifted my entire understanding of family.

I was at a conference, a Family Teams weekend. It was not simply meant to be an experience of information but rather a transformation as we worked intentionally on our families. The first message of the weekend began with the same challenge I just gave you—define *family*.

That should have been so simple for me. My role in ministry at the time was the family life pastor at a local church. I had developed strategies for marriage, parenting, child development, and counseling to guide and coach families through all of life's stages. I had just completed my Master's of theology and had attended countless conference sessions and breakouts to discover and develop family resources. More importantly, I was the father of four children and married to an amazing woman who had journeyed with me to develop a great family. She sat by my side as we tried to write a definition of family.

We stared at the page and then at each other. We tried to verbally process this, but everything we said seemed to fall short. I was dumbfounded. How had I jumped to developing strategies and resources without a clear definition of what I was trying to assess? Everything I came up with seemed too small and incomplete or too complicated and wordy, which left me less than inspired. I was operating in an assumed definition that had been built through my Western cultural experience and mindset. I realized in that moment that almost everyone has an assumed but underdeveloped definition of family.

Your definition has been formed through a combination of family of origin and cultural experience. The majority of our definitions for family are caught rather than taught. I grew up in central Kentucky in an area that held family in high regard but, like most Western cultures, lacked any true definition or guiding vision for this good intention. When you ask Siri to define *family*, you will get a long list of definitions that begins with a group consisting of parents and children living together in a household. Or my personal favorite is a group of people united in criminal activity. In his book *Family Revision*, Jeremy Pryor breaks down the common Western definition of family as essentially a nurturing environment that provides a springboard for individual success.

How close is this to the definition you wrote earlier? This definition is actually accurate when I think of what we are trying to create in Western family culture. We tend to reduce the idea of family to a nuclear experience that begins when a man and a woman get married and have children. Some consider them a new family when they get married, but some simply refer to them as a couple until they add one to two and a half children to the nest. This definition is predicated on the value of autonomous individualism, which basically means I don't need anyone's help to live my personal dreams. The goal of family is reduced to building stronger individuals to better support the culture of individualism we exist in. There are many dangers to this definition that I don't intend to fully unpack here, but some notable oversights are singles and grandparents. Are they still part of a family? Is there any possibility of a lasting legacy or heritage?

This shortsighted view of a nurturing nest has led to its own unintended consequences of brokenness in the Western family experience. Our pursuit of individual happiness has led to a growing disillusionment with marriage and family. After decades of declining marriage rates and changes in family structure, the share of American adults who have never been married is at an historical high. In 2012, one-in-five adults ages 25 and older (about 42 million people) had never been married, according to a Pew Research Center analysis of census data.[3] In 1960, only about one in 10 adults (9 percent) in that age range had never been married. Many researchers are pointing to a declining or leveling off of our current divorce rate but fail to link the significant decline of new marriages with that statistic. The United States has the highest rate of children living in single parent homes by a significant margin of 23 percent. A staggering two-thirds of people ages 18–29 and more than half of those ages 30–49 expressed that other priorities are more important than marriage and children. The greatest priority seems to be individual happiness, yet the highest rate of depression is found in the 18–29 age range. Depression and suicide rates are consistently linked to social isolation, loneliness, and instability. What if chasing individual happiness doesn't actually lead to lasting fulfillment?

Most church and family strategies keep trying to patch holes in a ship that is taking on water and headed in the wrong direction. What if we look at the ancient and biblical definition of family as a better and lasting foundation? What has stood the test of time? What leads to greater stability and legacy?

This is what the LORD says:
"Stand at the crossroads and look;
ask for the ancient paths,
ask where the good way is, and walk in it,
and you will find rest for your souls."

—Jer. 6:16

Not surprisingly, there have been many iterations of family in various centuries and civilizations. From tribalism to hyperindividualism, families have experienced blessings and challenges based on their shared view of this basic institution.

I could give many cultural examples, but Jewish families have notably retained their identities through centuries of intense challenges and struggles. They trace their definition of family to the story of and generational connection to Father Abraham. In the book of Genesis, God selects Abram (his previous name) to bless and bring blessing to the whole world. God promises him this in his old age:

I will make you into a great nation,
and I will bless you;
I will make your name great,
and you will be a blessing.
I will bless those who bless you,
and whoever curses you I will curse;
and all peoples on earth
will be blessed through you.

—Gen. 12:2–3

This promise seemed impossible since Abram and his wife were really old and had zero descendants. However, Abram believed

18

God was capable of building a great nation, making his name great, and blessing him even though Abram was unable to achieve or see it in his lifetime. He sacrificed his short-term, individual, and immediate desires to embrace God's promise of a generational vision. God changed Abram's name to Abraham, which means "father of many nations." Abraham viewed his descendants as the vehicle of the vision of blessing God had spoken over him. This willingness to sacrifice and steward the remaining years of his life to enable this vision is best described in the book of Hebrews.

> *By faith Abraham, when called to go to a place he would later receive as his inheritance, obeyed and went, even though he did not know where he was going. By faith he made his home in the promised land like a stranger in a foreign country; he lived in tents, as did Isaac and Jacob, who were heirs with him of the same promise. For he was looking forward to the city with foundations, whose architect and builder is God.*

—Heb. 11:8–10

The city God was building through the family lineage of Abraham is still standing and was promised to stand for eternity to come. The vision of Abraham was to develop an enduring family that all people on earth would be blessed by. This blessing was extended through Abraham's son Isaac, his grandson Jacob, and countless other descendants as they carried forward the identity and mission God gave their family. In Hebrew, *family* means "joined together." This definition illustrates a deep, interdependent connection shared through blood lines and generations carrying a family name and mission forward. Abraham's individual experience of family was challenging and sacrificial, but it laid a framework for a simpler and longer-lasting definition of family.

Family Is a Multigenerational Team on a Mission

A team. Wearing the same jersey. Connected and depending on each other. Encouraging each other to grow and develop for the benefit of the team. A multigenerational team has an identity and purpose. The family name encourages honor and legacy. Resources in a multigenerational team are stewarded to experience the broader blessing for the family and surrounding community. The values of the team and lasting connectedness are reinforced through gatherings and traditions. Different gifts and passions are celebrated as potential expansions of the mission of the family team.

In this multigenerational team model of family, we find inspiration to give up short-term personal gain for a longer-lasting and more transcendent cause. Abraham and his children lived like foreigners in tents in the new land they were promised to possess much later. We also see enduring faith in God's greater vision as Abraham passed down this promise and identity to his descendants to live as the people of God. The generational blessing is developed throughout the Bible as this line of descendants leads to the line of Davidic kings and ultimately to Jesus, the King of kings. He would invite people from every tribe, tongue, and nation to be adopted into the everlasting multi-ethnic family of God.

You may be thinking, *Wait! I'm not Abraham. I don't think my family will impact all people on earth.* First, I would encourage you to be careful not to limit what is possible generationally. We serve a great God who sees much farther than we do. He makes amazing things happen two and three generations after revealing His vision. Second, seek to live out the mission your family team is uniquely crafted by God to fulfill. Too many families stumble trying to live out the mission of some other family. God has a plan for you and your family. Live that plan.

Nuclear Family Fallout

Viewing family as a multigenerational team is not a new concept. It has stood as the definition of family throughout ancient and classical civilizations. By contrast, the nuclear family model is barely entering its toddler phase. The fallout of this individualized model of family is significant since it decreases the desire for familial bonds and deepens the relational divide to encourage independent mindsets.

In the nuclear family model, previous generations are forgotten as each new generation seeks to build a new individual identity based on their performance and production. Honor and connectedness are only viewed as aspirational characteristics if they benefit the pursuit of the individual. Lasting meaning and identity are repeatedly lost, but each newly established nuclear family thinks they can do better and that their individual love will be enough to carry them through the challenges of life and keep them together. They won't make the same mistakes their parents made, yet the treadmill seems to get faster, and the broken pieces keep piling up. Grandparents often move on to experience their golden years in isolation as they watch their children raise their grandchildren from the sidelines and just purchase gifts for birthdays and holidays.

Instead, imagine your great-great-great-great-grandchildren experiencing the blessings of purpose, connectedness, and legacy because of the time you spent developing the foundations of a multigenerational family team. God crafted your family with a purpose, and He wants to lead you with an enduring mission that will bless your current experience of family and your future family in ways you cannot currently imagine. How can you transition away from this Western mindset of family to the ancient and biblical mindset behind family? I'm glad you asked.

Transition

Moving to a multigenerational team experience of family requires several paradigm shifts in your thinking. The team mindset literally changes everything when you begin to see family through this lens. Our thinking results in doing in most situations. So with each fundamental concept, we will discuss the battleground of change, beginning with paradigms to believe, and then move to practices to apply. Here is what has been a revolutionary verse in the Bible for my journey.

> *Do not conform to the pattern of this world, but be transformed by the renewing of your mind. Then you will be able to test and approve what God's will is—his good, pleasing and perfect will.*

—Rom. 12:2

We all have a tendency to conform to the pattern of those around us. Even if the results are disastrous, we (like lemmings) keep jumping off the same dangerous cliff. However, Paul challenges us to be transformed by the renewing of, or changing of, our minds to be aligned with truth. As our minds are renewed and built up with conviction to live a new path forward, we have the courage to make different decisions in order to experience God's will and vision for our lives. One important paradigm to shift as we attempt to understand the biblical mindset is to think communally, not individually. When we see the word *you*, we naturally think of the individual you, but this verse, like many in Scripture, uses a plural pronoun. Since I grew up in central Kentucky, I often replace *you* with *y'all*.

Y'all need to transform your thinking to know and experience God's mission and plan for y'all's life. It's so much better than the world's way around, y'all.

—Rom. 12:2 (DHV, Daniel's (my) Hillbilly Version)

God's plan for your family is good, pleasing, and perfect. How much would change in your experience if you really believed God had your best path forward? How would y'all change if you knew and lived out His will? It is a better way than the one the world is offering. His way is an unchanging call to the great commandment to love God and love others as He has loved you. Let's look at the key paradigms that need to change in our thinking about family as a team.

Nest vs. Team (Independent vs. Interdependent)

The nest has been used as a primary family metaphor in the Western world. Thinking of family as a nest for baby birds may have limited merit for understanding child development, but it has several negative connotations. Mama bird makes a soft nest for helpless baby birds. Mama feeds the birds until they are strengthened enough to attempt to fly on their own. Progressively, the comfortable and soft aspects of the nest are removed to cause the baby birds to test out their wings. The goal of the nest is to strengthen individual bird development until they can fly out, independent of Mama or the other birds.

23

Is this really the vision you have for your family—disconnected individuals living their own lives? It's basically investing 18 years of sacrificial time, money, and energy into your child's life and then watching them drive away and say, "Thanks, Mom. I might see you again someday." Is the goal of family simply to launch individuals? Is it a failure if they return to the nest? Developing confidence and life skills is really important, but even birds look for connection as they fly in flocks. Is Mama bird's goal to get the birds raised so she can go back to living and providing for herself? Are the golden years of retirement meant to be lived in isolation?

Here's another important question. Where's Daddy bird? Many men struggle to find their roles in the nurturing environment of the nest. They often give the best of themselves to their work as an attempt to provide for the physical needs of the nest. However, this leads to greater emotional and relational disconnection with the family since shared memories are in short supply. Dads are chastened by the culture for not investing more time at home, but they are continually pushed to make more money in order to give more opportunity to their baby birds' autonomous futures.

A team casts an entirely different vision than a nest. Imagine for a moment that your family team competes weekly against other family teams with results posted online. Let's use the example of your family as a soccer team since it's the most played and watched sport in the world. It's also really convenient since I have played and coached soccer for decades.

How would you approach life differently as a family? Would you have regular practices and training? The team would need to be prepared in the skills necessary for each position. Individuals would be developed to fulfill their roles on the team. Everyone

24

would depend on each other and encourage each person's development for the good of the team. When a player scored or the goalie saved an opponent's shot, the whole team would celebrate. Conversely, if one player went down with an injury, the entire team would feel the loss.

The focus of the nest is independence, while the concept of a team is interdependency. Independence can help cast vision in developing skills, but it lacks connectivity and meaning. Ironically, the well-trained, independent person leaves the nest looking for another group to connect to. We are designed for interdependence no matter how able we are to stand on our own two feet. Otherwise, we celebrate and struggle in isolation.

The team gives a lasting sense of connection as well as a long-term understanding of growth and development. It seems almost miraculous to watch a child go from tripping over the ball in a pack of five-year-olds to crossing a pass to a far post run for an aerial header. Only those who have witnessed the ups and downs of the journey can fully appreciate the developmental process. The team works together to help each member develop life skills. Reading, writing, math, and science are not something to individually score well in but rather beneficial abilities to add to the team for the greater good. This view of team leads to the next key paradigm shift for parents.

Chaperone vs. Coach (Outsourcing vs. Training)

Which term describes your role as a parent more completely—chaperone or coach? First, let's explore the role and ultimate goal of a chaperone. The goal of a chaperone is to make sure everyone is safe and alive and to ensure they don't dance too closely at the middle school dance. The chaperone has very little responsibility other than to watch from the side and remind people of the rules when they break them or get close to breaking them. This role matches much of Western parenting since it is more convenient to have others focus on skill-, social-, spiritual-, and knowledge-based development. We have a tendency to let the professionals do the teaching and training while we do our best to transport our children to all these activities and make sure they get fed and in bed. Teachers, youth pastors, coaches, daycare workers, and counselors are believed to be better equipped (often in larger groups of children) to meet the needs of our kids than we are. Chaperones rarely attempt to offer advice or training as they attempt to get through their limited hours of engagement.

Coaches do not approach their teams in the same manner. I coach a combination of new and returning soccer teams each year. With my new teams, I have to learn each player's strengths and weaknesses as quickly as possible. Then it is urgent to develop the weak areas and find the best position for their strengths in order to benefit the team. Teaching and training the fundamentals of passing and dribbling expose these opportunities and develop the future plan for training sessions. The team grows throughout the season but only leaves me wishing I could keep building on what was established.

Returning teams are an entirely different experience. As we begin our first practice of the season, I already know all the players' names, strengths, weaknesses, and natural positioning. It's fun to see a growth spurt or an increase in strength between seasons. We pick up where we left off and keep developing chemistry in passing through movement with and without the ball. Skills are in continual development, and ongoing jokes and stories from last season add to the environment of friendship and teamwork. An extra player or two may add to the strength of the team, but they need to build relational and on-field trust from the returning players.

As a coach, I am always looking to develop, grow, and position players for the good of the team. I see a direct connection between our practices and our performance on game day. That builds urgency and importance behind every minute of our time together. The success of the team often depends on the dedication and development of each player who is impacted most by the role of the coach. The coach cannot take the place of players, but focused preparation will set players up for the greatest opportunities for success.

In a team-based family mindset, parents are meant to function in a coaching role. The parent develops each child and looks for his or her natural strengths. Some strengths will be obvious from an early age, while others will appear over time. Skill development takes precedence over the common digital pacifiers. The goal of the parent is not to simply keep the child occupied but to realize his or her full potential. The coach is not expected to be an expert in every aspect of life. However, the coach takes ownership for seeking out beneficial training environments to encourage players in continual growth. The goal is not to simply get children fed and in bed but to make the most of training opportunities together to grow physically, spiritually, emotionally, relationally, and mentally. These trainings come as you look for simple opportunities along the way to improve basic routines with intentionality (see Deut. 11:19). They will also come as you shift your focus to the following paradigm.

Quick and Fleeting vs. Deep and Meaningful (Fading vs. Lasting)

Have you seen the newest viral video? Have you listened to the top hit single? Did you read the tweet? Catch my story update? Binge the brand-new series? There is so much competing for our attention that it feels like we are too busy and overburdened to keep up. We naturally try to be in the know with everyone else, but it feels like we skip across the surface on digital jet skis trying to keep up with the ever-changing stream. It's interesting, however, that all these new and viral options don't seem to last beyond their trendy moment of popularity.

In our modern culture, there is little that lasts. We are consumed with the quick and fleeting, and we often miss the deep and meaningful. It is notable that much of what is regularly shared on social media today fades in a short time as a story update instead of a lasting post. More publishing tools, filters, and edits are possible today than ever before. Yet there is a fascination with music, movies, stories, and practices of the past as something deeper and more meaningful.

How can you move to spending more time and focus on the lasting aspects of life? Deep and meaningful moments are often creative and communal. When a team builds something together, serves alongside each other, or completes a task utilizing each person's skill and contribution, the team remembers it. There are projects worth working hard on together in order to build teamwork and skills. Sharing family stories and experiences and connecting deeply in an unhurried manner give life to the family team.

There are also meaningful repetitions that need to be emphasized time and again in order to keep them at the forefront of our minds. In his book *Think Orange*, Reggie Joiner reminds families to say less more often so everyone knows what really matters. As we will discuss in the next chapter, your family should know the mission, purpose, and unique identity of your family.

What are you doing or developing now that will matter 10, 20, or 100 years later? What would it look like to move more time into the deep, meaningful, and lasting category? How could you opt out of portions of modern culture's quick and fleeting focus? Give yourself grace as you transition. Every moment doesn't have to be deep and meaningful, but focus your mind on building toward these opportunities.

Peer-Based Identity vs. Foundational Family Identity (Finding vs. Reminding)

Teenagers are encouraged to find themselves. They are challenged to discover their identity, sexuality, and purpose in this life. While there are potentially liberating emotions, the primary pursuit can only be found in performance and comparison. The next generation has been sent on a quest to find their identities based on how they measure up to or relate to their peers. Parents have been encouraged not to influence the spiritual, mental, or even gender perspective of their children in order to encourage their self-actualization. However, this identity is not built in a cave as an individual; it is realized in a communal way as children perceive their value based on the responses of their surrounding peers. The response is almost always a reaction of approval based again on performance, appearance, or popularity. In a desire to be known and loved by their peers, children will act as social chameleons until they find an accepting and affirming group.

This core question is to be wrestled with: Is it more beneficial to achieve a peer-based identity or to remind yourself of a foundational family identity? In a healthy family environment, a child has grown up in an environment of acceptance that isn't based on achievement. The child is known and loved for who they are, not what they do. Accomplishment doesn't increase love and acceptance but is celebrated by the team as a victory. The child seeks to honor the investment of generations in developing a heritage worthy of respect. Risk is possible through the security of foundational love and support that is not dependent on performance. Modern psychologists and theologians still agree that attachment to a strong foundational family experience is beneficial to development.

In peer-based identity, you must achieve and discover an identity based on performance and comparison. While peer-based comparison is a natural part of development, family has the opportunity to provide a safety net of acceptance, love, and security. When your teen doesn't feel they measure up "out there," they can be assured that they are valued "in here." In a foundational family identity, a child is reminded of his or her value and worth as an interdependent member of a multigenerational team. Individual growth is accelerated and celebrated in this environment of security and acceptance. The child's development does not just benefit the child's position with peers; it extends the family mission for generations to come. This enduring identity is found when a family team takes time to clarify its mission, meaning, and purpose. However, in order to truly stand the test of time, family identity must be wrapped in an eternal identity in Christ as recipients of grace and adoption into the family of God.

As you transition to this team mindset, you will be able to return to these ideas repeatedly in your family life. You will view your family through a new lens, and you will often assess the difficulties of life through these questions: Are we working together as a team? What skills can be developed to improve our team? What is bringing division to our team? As we assess the second fundamental of team, here is one of the most important questions you will ask as you evaluate decisions and priorities moving forward: How does this fit into our family mission?

Mission

Your family team has been uniquely crafted by God for a purpose. Everyone on the team needs to know the *why* behind what you do as a family. Ephesians 2:10 reminds us that "we are God's handiwork, created in Christ Jesus to do good works, which God prepared in advance for us to do." Discovering your specific family mission can feel like a daunting task, but it is usually achieved with some research and by answering a few key questions. Most importantly, it begins with asking God to guide you to the specific plan He has for your family. Invite other family members to join you as you listen for His clarifying voice.

At a men's conference early in my new role as a father, I was challenged to establish a family mission statement. That was a totally new concept for me and for many of the men in the room. We knew the mission statement for the businesses or organizations we worked for, but few of us had a vision for the family God had entrusted to us. We all prayed and asked God for wisdom as we wrote down a few key values we wanted to be true of our families. Then we took this home and invited our spouses to join us as we worked on our family mission statements. After a lot of conversation about our ultimate desires for our family and guiding values for the character we hoped to embody, we landed on a family mission for the McKees.

The McKees Exist to Know God and Make Him Known through Loving, Serving, and Giving

We loved that we came to a conclusion, and we still stand on that foundational mission for our family. The key values of loving, serving, and giving were unpacked further through a list of scriptures to know what love and humility look like on a practical level. We began to teach this to our young kids who recited them with pretty solid accuracy. We developed a team cheer that ended with Love, Serve, Give! We were so excited about this foundational truth that could be repeated for generations to come. We thought our team mission was complete, but God had more depth to build into it.

After the Family Teams conference, we were inspired to keep pursuing our mission more intentionally as a family. We invited our kids into the process and asked their perspectives as we journeyed together. We began to discuss more questions about our family name, so I began to research the meaning of our last name. It was a powerful moment to discover that McKee means "fire." That fire metaphor kept presenting itself over and over in that season.

The previous month, someone had shared a vision of me tending a fire and embers rising from my fire to start other fires. I believed this was directly tied to the men's retreat I had just led where men gathered around fires to share their stories, struggles, and faith journeys. I was so excited about the idea of fire as a place of warmth and light for men to find healing and direction for their lives. However, God had an even bigger vision for these men—to tend the fires of their families and keep developing generational legacy. This grew my passion and depth for our family mission even more and led to more research. We learned of our Scottish ancestry and the sacrificial journey to bring our family to America. This depth developed a greater vision than our individual family and built gratitude for the deep and meaningful aspects of family we had missed all along.

Our children now repeat with us regularly the meaning of our family name and mission.

What does McKee mean?
Fire

What does fire produce?
Light, warmth, and forever change.

How do we change things forever?
The McKees exist to know God and make Him known through loving, serving, and giving.

This identity for our family is aspirational and secure. The mission is clear and focuses on the lasting character and goals of our family. I do not share this to encourage you to copy this mission as your own. Actually, one of the great enemies of discovering your family mission is comparison, which will cause you to try to live out another family's story when God uniquely crafted you as His workmanship. We want to help you discover *your* family mission.

Your family mission is better discovered than invented. The statement you develop should be an attempt to better articulate what already exists in your family heritage, gifting, and unique makeup. There are many potential paths to this discovery process, but utilizing these questions and prompts should help move you forward in developing your family team mission.

Start with Vision

Work through these questions individually, and then discuss together with your spouse or another family member to discover similarities and shared passion areas.

What do you hope the reality of your family 10 years from now will be? Describe each of these aspects of your family:

Marriage
Children
Extended family
Home environment (culture and character)

As you discuss this future reality of your family with your spouse or family member, what stands out?

What would be an added vision of your family if you extended it 20 years?

Problem-Solvers

God designed your family to journey together with Him to redeem and restore the world to its original design. The prayer modeled for us by Jesus is to invite God's kingdom to come and His will to be done on earth as it is in heaven. We co-labor with God in this restorative process by recognizing our gifting and engaging the brokenness around us.

- What do you do well? How are you uniquely gifted?
- What bothers you about the world?
- How could your family be used to help restore a broken aspect of the world?

Past, Present, Pillars

Past

Your family did not begin with you. You have a name and heritage that stood long before you joined the legacy. As we discussed in the first chapter, there will always be a gap between your ideal and real family experience. However, there is often depth of meaning, heroic stories, and family identity to be discovered as we look to our past.

- What does your last name mean? What is the history, origin, or metaphor associated with it?
- What is an inspirational story or idea about one of your ancestors?
- What countries or regions of the world have your ancestors lived in?

Present

You are currently in a specific location, in a specific family season, and you have a unique opportunity to make a lasting impact. It is important to recognize the opportunities and honest challenges of this season of your family's life. Many families imagine a time when everything will be easier and more conducive to making their ideal impact and miss the current opportunities around them. The best way to make a better future is to start by clarifying small ways to make the world better today.

- What do you love about the place you currently live in?
- How could you bless someone else around you today?
- How could you use this unique season to make a positive impact on others?

- How could current resources be aligned or generously given to make an impact?

Pillars

Another way to discover a memorable family mission is to first develop the pillars or key values on which your family will stand. Declaring the priorities and character qualities of your family will guide you in decision-making and regular discipline opportunities.

- What are your family's top five priorities? Rank them in order of importance.
- What are the top five character qualities you hope to see displayed in your family?
- What are the top five characteristics you don't want to be true of your family?

Enjoy discovering your family mission together! Don't work in isolation. Invite others into the process to establish a shared passion and well-rounded mission statement.

Meditate on this psalm as you process and pray through God's unique design and direction for your family.

> *Unless the LORD builds the house,*
>   *the builders labor in vain.*
> *Unless the LORD watches over the city,*
>   *the guards stand watch in vain.*
> *In vain you rise early*
>   *and stay up late,*
> *toiling for food to eat—*
>   *for he grants sleep to those he loves.*
> *Children are a heritage from the LORD,*
>   *offspring a reward from him.*
> *Like arrows in the hands of a warrior*
>   *are children born in one's youth.*
> *Blessed is the man*
>   *whose quiver is full of them.*
> *They will not be put to shame*
>   *when they contend with their opponents in court.*

—Ps. 127

3

Time

Rhythm

*A*METRONOME IS A device used by a composer to set the rhythm of a musical piece through a measurement of beats per minute, or BPM. Before reading ahead, grab a device or computer and type "metronome" into the search engine. (Bonus points: If you have an actual metronome, grab it instead.) You should see a digital metronome show up at 100 BPM. Play that first to feel a steady beat. Next, slide the scale to 150 BPM, and play it again. How does that feel different? What does this BPM do to your pulse and emotions? Finally, slide the scale down to 50 BPM. Now what do you feel? It's crazy how a simple change of tempo can impact you physically and emotionally.

When the speed slows down, the clicking may begin to relax you, and you might enjoy it, but others may feel more anxious and demand that the beat speed up. Is this thing ever going to click? What's interesting to me is that almost every family has someone wanting to speed it up and another wanting to slow it down. If you had to choose a current BPM to characterize the rhythm of your family schedule, what would it be? What would you like your tempo to be?

We live in a universe defined by rhythm. As you inhale and exhale, your breathing has rhythm. Your heart beats in rhythm, and you have brainwaves that move in rhythm. Sunrise and sunset consistently return in a stunning daily display. The seasons move forward in a quarterly rhythm of growth and rest. Winter brings snow for the mountains of Yosemite, and summer yields beautiful cascading waterfalls as the snowpack melts away. Farming has a rhythm of sowing, growing, and harvesting. The ocean waves crash resoundingly constant as the tide comes in and goes out.

Every Family Has a Unique Rhythm

You have a one-of-a-kind family and a unique rhythm. There may be similarities with others around you, but no one does life exactly like you do. You have unique challenges and opportunities with your work, home, family, and community responsibilities. Your breakfast and bedtime routines may be quirky, but they are distinctively yours. You face daily battles that others don't have to fight, and they wear on your resolve to keep going. Your unique family rhythm reveals a great deal about who you are and what you value.

Although you are a unique snowflake of a family, is it possible that many of the issues you experience may be less a personnel problem and more a rhythm problem? It's easy to look around for someone to blame for regular frustrations, but maybe you're simply stuck in a flow of time that isn't producing life, purpose, and joy. An inconsistency between your desires and reality are at times easily resolved by assessing your schedules and routines. You may have visions of great family dinner conversations, but you rarely sit around your table together. Or maybe there is a desire to serve others, but these opportunities don't find their way into the schedule.

There are many opportunities we don't experience because of our tightly packed schedules. The experiences we do share as a family are drastically impacted by a lack of margin or breathing room in our schedules. Imagine your family getting ready for school after everyone got up a little later than usual. You have to finish getting ready and yell—or loudly instruct everyone—to make sure they're ready because you are running late. When you make it to the door, backpacks aren't ready, breakfast is scattered across the kitchen, kids are on devices, and shoes are lost in the abyss of your home. You threaten—or lovingly remind—everyone to get ready as quickly as possible, and through a frantic miracle, you make it out the door three minutes behind schedule. You might make it, but probably not. Buckle up, everyone. The drive is filled with responsibility reminders, inconvenient red lights, terrible drivers, and boiling frustration for everyone in the car.

Okay, that was terrible. Now go back through the entire experience, and add 15 to 20 minutes. How would extra time change every interaction? How would you view the inconveniences differently? In what ways could you bring encouragement and even enjoyment to the morning? What would be the attitude on the drive to school?

If you are like most families, you are currently living under the tyranny of the urgent. You may feel like most of your life is filled with endless have-to tasks and very few get-to opportunities. The requirements of work, meals, laundry, dishes, maintenance, bills, practices, and even bathing (when is the last time your children had baths?) feel overwhelming. There is never enough…time.

The BPM of your family rhythm may feel like it's more than 100, but why are you doing all you are currently doing? Who chose this schedule? How could some of your have-to obligations be transformed into get-to opportunities? What would it take to build your life around your clarified family mission?

Imagine if all of life stopped, you lost your job, and all of your responsibilities were wiped off of your schedule. Whoa! Hold up. Actually pause and process this potential reality for a minute.

What would you do with all of this Time?

Honestly, this is not hard to imagine as I write this book during the COVID-19 pandemic. After paying little attention to the news for a few days, I received an emergency alert on my phone while hiking with my family. The alert initiated a stay-at-home order that would begin the following day. Over the course of that evening and the next day, literally everything was canceled. Every event, practice, meeting, and friend's expectation was wiped clean off of the schedule. There was a great deal of scrambling to figure out life, and much of school and work moved to digital networking platforms, but all of a sudden there was...time. Time to choose what we wanted to do together. Time to assess our family and how we were really doing.

With this clean slate mindset, take some time to assess your family. Print off or pull out a blank weekly calendar, and use these questions to think through another possible rhythm.

- What are the top five things you wish were part of your weekly rhythm? Make a list on the side.
- From your list, what would you be most excited to write again on your blank schedule?
- What activity could you schedule to move your family mission into regular practice?
- What are truly necessary aspects of life you need to make time to do?
- If you assessed your normal rhythm, how many hours in a regular week are you actually together as a family? What would you like that number to be? What would be the best time slots for intentional family time?
- What would be the top three items from your previous rhythm that would not make it back on your blank schedule?

Several historical moments have demanded a total change in priorities. During times of war, entire nations have screeched to a halt, waiting anxiously for the outcome so they could resume life as either victors or subjugated servants. Christians in Rome transitioned in a single day out of running from persecution to opportunities for political power after Constantine converted to Christianity. The Israelites were led by Moses out of slavery in Egypt to become wanderers in the wilderness. Imagine that schedule.

"What are we doing today, Dad?"

"Following the cloud, Son, just waiting to see if it moves."

Switching to mom for better answers, "Where are we going, Mom?"

"Away from Egypt and to some land promised to us. We just have to be ready to keep moving, so make sure your things are ready. It could be today or another week or two."

No plan or schedule. Survive and advance to the next place God leads. After over 40 years of this, they transitioned from wanderers to warriors conquering the Promised Land. After God delivered the land to their possession, the Israelites found themselves with an incredible opportunity to live new lives as a free nation. Moses spoke in advance of this moment to guide the people and build a rhythm of life with God at the center.

Hear, O Israel: The LORD our God, the LORD is one. Love the LORD your God with all your heart and with all your soul and with all your strength. These commandments that I give you today are to be on your hearts. Impress them on your children. Talk about them when you sit at home and when you walk along the road, when you lie down and when you get up. Tie them as symbols on your hands and bind them on your foreheads. Write them on the doorframes of your houses and on your gates.

When the LORD your God brings you into the land he swore to your fathers, to Abraham, Isaac and Jacob, to give you—a land with large, flourishing cities you did not build, houses filled with all kinds of good things you did not provide, wells you did not dig, and vineyards and olive groves you did not plant—then when you eat and are satisfied, be careful that you do not forget the LORD, who brought you out of Egypt, out of the land of slavery.

—Deut. 6:4–12

The opening portion of this passage is called the *Shema*. This prayer has been one of the most influential traditions in Jewish history as it functioned both as the Jewish pledge of allegiance and a hymn of praise. This prayer was instituted as a morning and evening prayer in the daily rhythm of God's people. These simple words hold the capacity to reshape the course of an entire life by keeping love for and loyalty to God in the forefront of your mind. This prayer directs toward obedience, not out of obligation or duty, but out of love.

A Good Rhythm Requires a Director

You can't set up a nation without realizing who is in charge. A rhythm can't be built without a director or leader to set the pace. Here are some questions for your family: Who has set the rhythm for your family? Is it the kids? Work? The culture around you? There is a huge competition for your heart, your money, and your time. God called His people to love Him first and follow His commands because He knew it was for their good. To experience life that is truly life together, they would have to submit to someone who had a greater vantage point and a greater love for everyone as a whole than one specific individual following their wants and feelings. Every one of us has a desire to be the director and decide what *we* do with *our* time. However, when we submit our rhythm to His leadership, we experience direction and confidence to live for something greater than ourselves.

Let's be honest, are you really the best guide for your personal use of time? Or do you have a tendency like all of us to coast or justify your use of extra time and money on yourself? We have a tendency, like the Deuteronomy passage states, to forget—to forget who our time and resources come from and who they are ultimately for. Anytime we find ourselves coasting or in default mode, it usually doesn't result in great things. You don't usually hear these statements:

- "It's amazing! I just woke up stronger, and the fat fell right off."
- "We just let everyone do what they want, and we are all happier and healthier."
- "I increased my hours playing video games, and our family relationships couldn't be better."
- "Our family spends hours isolated on screens in different rooms, and we are changing the world together."

We spend a lot of time doing what is neither meaningful nor enjoyable. We coast into the cultural pattern around us and move toward nothingness. We easily become experts at spending our time on pointless apps and reading the same news and social media feeds repeatedly. We are the first generation truly in danger of entertaining ourselves to death. The battle for our attention and desire to escape into nothingness is actually really powerful, but it's not new. Check out this quote from *The Screwtape Letters* by C. S. Lewis, published in 1942: "Nothing is very strong: strong enough to steal away a man's best years not in sweet sins but in a dreary flickering of the mind over it knows not what and knows not why."[4]

Nothing, not just outright intentional sin, has the power to steal your best years and replace them with regret. An easy test for the time you spend is if you are glad to share your use of time with a mentor. Our time and priorities are meant to reflect the Shema and point to the divine wisdom of God and His leadership in our lives. That is why Paul challenges Christ-followers to watch their time and lives closely.

Be very careful, then, how you live—not as unwise but as wise, making the most of every opportunity, because the days are evil. Therefore do not be foolish, but understand what the Lord's will is.

—Eph. 5:15-17

There is a use of time that is wise and a use that is unwise. The days of life are presented as evil in two primary ways. First, in the immediate context, Paul draws a distinction between living in the light and living in darkness. The evil days are a combination of the default mode of the world around us and the selfish tendencies inside of us. We can easily get caught up in the flow of intentional evil, but even more subtly we find the second evil. The days of life pass quickly. We must make the most of every opportunity because the opportunities we plan to get to later will never happen. This evil is found in the regret and meaninglessness into which we can unwisely drift. Instead, we build our lives around the invitation to know and experience God's will for our lives—His good, pleasing, and perfect will (Rom. 12:2). So watch your family life closely because your rhythm teaches more to your kids and the people around you about what you value than what you intend.

Now that you know your family mission and team purpose, it is *time* to change the way you think about your *time*.

Intentional

There is power in deciding in advance and purposely scheduling key priorities for your family. Families must *aim* their time at their mission. If you are willing to intentionally look at your rhythm and build your family life around your mission, you will be blown away at the results. It all begins with rethinking a few key paradigms about time and change.

Assess

The first step in aiming your time toward your mission is to assess. In his famous philosophical quote, Socrates challenged everyone to pause and look at their lives, stating, "The unexamined life is not worth living."[5] If you are willing to honestly assess your family life, you have the potential to shift the course of your future. We often avoid this due to good intentions and well-formed excuses. Our life experience has a way of helping us overlook the reality of our family life. However, if we are ready to truly assess and move forward, it begins with this simple question:

How are we really doing?

It's not how we want to be doing or how we should be doing. It's how we are really doing. Do we actually spend enough time together to live as a connected team? Take this important question through categories to develop key priorities for your family. It's usually best to start with an assessment of the whole family and then work with each individual member to understand them. Some categories that are usually helpful to apply are the five key areas of life: physical, relational, emotional, spiritual, mental-skill development. Humans are a complicated combination of body, soul, and spirit with needs in each of these five key areas.

Physical – Are we able to physically accomplish what we want to accomplish? Do we keep fitness, sleep, and healthy eating as a priority in our family? What area needs growth?

Relational – How are the relationships in our home? Is there an underlying tension that needs to be dealt with? Do we have healthy friendships outside of our family? Are we regularly enjoying time together as a family? What relationships need the most attention?

Emotional – What is the overall emotional temperature of our home? Is it hot in boiling conflict or cold in isolation and secrecy? Are we motivated toward good desires and family connection? Are we able to engage in healthy conflict? Is there an instability that needs to be addressed?

Spiritual – Is our faith taking the priority in our home that we desire? Does faith practice feel like an essential part of our family or an add-on to weekly activities? What would it practically look like to grow in this area? How can serving others become a regular priority?

Mental-Skill – Are we growing in the areas of knowledge and skill development? What is the ratio of time spent consuming media focused on the skills and knowledge of others to developing our own skills and knowledge? What growth areas are the priority to help accomplish our family mission?

Honestly answering questions like these will help you achieve a more accurate picture of the current state of your family. This process needs to serve as an affirmation of the good and a wake-up call to the needs of your family. Try to spend more time celebrating the good in your current situation than just criticizing your struggles. It is important to avoid the good-bad split that leads us to either gloss over the needs or forget the blessings in our current reality. As you evaluate, look more through the lens of the whole family as a team to encourage interdependence than processing individually toward independence. Other areas that may be beneficial to assess are financial, marriage, and specific priorities of your family mission.

Integrate

After assessing your rhythm, celebrating your strengths, and finding key areas of growth, realistically integrate these growth areas in order to further your family mission. Your assessment must bring change to the schedule or else growth will stagnate as another good intention that was never realized. These decisions of integration will guide you to say yes to growth and no to misaligned opportunities. Can you stay after work to help with a special project? Will you volunteer to lead the decorating team? We are offering your child a spot on an elite team. Will you accept? We can make more progress if we move this to a weekly meeting. Does that work for you? The people-pleaser in all of us wants to say yes when we're asked to do something.

The decisions of life are not usually between good opportunities and blatant sinful activity but between competing priorities. Even good desires can be destructive when they crowd out the more important momentum toward your shared family mission. Simply put, every time you say yes, you are also saying no. The most valuable asset of life is time. It has been said that the best way to spell love is T-I-M-E. You cannot produce more time, and once it is spent, it can never be recovered. We often approach the sands of time like a sandbox instead of an hourglass. We love to believe we can move time around and always have excess for needs that arise. It doesn't really matter how we choose to use it because there is more available. An hourglass is pretty sobering, however. Once one grain of sand falls from the top to the bottom, it no longer has the potential to go back to the top and be used again. Unlike the little one-minute hourglass timer, we don't get to flip the hourglass of life over.

As you evaluate decisions for your family, make sure to understand the no behind the yes. If you want more time, freedom, and energy for your family mission, start saying no to lesser things. Every yes has a list of competing priorities that we are refusing. The biblical concept to grow in the character of Christ and live in our new identity is found in this challenge from Paul in his letter to the Ephesians.

> *You were taught, with regard to your former way of life, to put off your old self, which is being corrupted by its deceitful desires; to be made new in the attitude of your minds; and to put on the new self, created to be like God in true righteousness and holiness.*

—Eph. 4:22-24

Life change takes an intentional putting off or removing of old practices and putting on or replacing them with new attitudes and identity. This remove-and-replace concept applies directly to our schedules as well. We must honestly look at what needs to be removed in order to replace them with focused momentum toward the life we want to live. No has the ability to open the door for a better yes. One exercise that can prove beneficial in this process is called Start, Stop, Keep. Essentially, it is a tool to evaluate your current reality with a new practice to say yes to, an old practice to say no to, and a current practice to keep saying yes to due to its effectiveness.

Micro Moves

Your first temptation when assessing your rhythm and integrating change may be to quit everything to make macro or large-scale change. You might think, "If we stop eating and sleeping, we will have so much time! Problem solved." Or you might use this moment as an excuse to enforce the end of everyone's extracurricular activities. Just as a fad diet and New Year's resolutions usually fall flat, so do attempts to change everything in a moment. Your rhythm may require a couple macro moves to bring significant change to your use of time as a family, but micro moves have even more power over time to bring lasting change. Let's be honest. Change is hard. Change comes through two types of motivation—extrinsic (external rewards) and intrinsic (personal desire). External rewards can be useful to encourage the crucial first steps, but a shared desire for growth to accomplish your family mission is necessary for lasting change. Drawing your family into the conversation about mission, goals, and priorities with initial rewards has the potential to increase motivation away from the current state toward growth in key areas.

It's important that you don't try to change everything all at once but rather enhance your rhythm with fun and build excitement around new shared priorities of your family. To grow spiritually as a family, it may be beneficial to build a weekly memory verse or breakfast Bible time into your rhythm. Reward yourselves with a weekly prize or earned income for memorizing a verse. Relationally you might find growth in family connection through playing a group game together after dinner once a week. Post a weekly winner chart, or write it on a family whiteboard or chalkboard. Physically you may want to choose a couple nights a week for exercise and activity over passive media consumption. Once you declare Moving Mondays or Fitness

Fridays for your family, it will become as normal as brushing your teeth. The easiest way to motivate in areas of physical or skill development is to train for a specific event or performance that you schedule on the calendar. Deadlines and specific goals move good intentions into action and make the micro moves of change feel worth the effort. In his book *The Common Rule*, Justin Earley reminds us, "Habits form much more than our schedules: they form our hearts."[6]

We often overestimate what is possible in short-term change and underestimate the potential of long-term consistency. These micro moves develop a long walk in the same direction that leads to a stability of identity and practice that becomes foundational for each family member. In the book *How People Grow*, Henry Cloud and John Townsend lay out these three primary ingredients of growth: relationship, truth, and time. As we grow in relationship to God and others, renew our minds with truth and an honest assessment of reality, and consistently apply these practices, over time we will experience a harvest of blessing.

Margin

Remember our opening illustration about the rush to get out the door for school? Think about your character in that process. Do you like the rushed version of you? Truth be told, no one enjoys the character or results of a rushed person or product. Yet we keep increasing the pace in order to produce and accomplish more each minute while missing the enjoyment of any real moments. Wayne Muller, mentor, therapist, and minister, said, "We have forgotten what enough feels like. We live in a world seduced by its own unlimited potential."[7] The possibilities of our time are unlimited in productivity and connectivity, but how much is enough? When do we stop? Why do we feel exhausted so often with so many tools for convenience?

Do you have any margin? Or are you living at the teetering edge of time and capacity? Take a full 30 seconds right now to put down the book and breathe deeply. Set a timer, and let oxygen hit the full capacity of your lungs.

How did that feel? Or did you skip past it and promise yourself you will do it later? When we pause and create margin, we bring a better and healthier version of ourselves to the situations we face. Unhurried living restores a sense of satisfaction and joy in work and relationships. Margin can only be created in modern times through intentionally disconnecting from our devices and pausing our potential productivity. Creating moments of margin will give you time to be fully present where you are. These moments often lead to clarity for the work you get to do and allow the desire to escape into entertainment to decrease.

We must relentlessly pursue an unhurried life or all the margin will be filled with endless activity and others' attempts to gain our attention. Space at the beginning of the day to pray and seek God's direction for the hours ahead has the power to transform the experience of every following moment. Now let's discuss the greatest practice to create and experience the blessing of margin and rest.

Sabbath

The reality of rhythm traces its roots all the way back to creation. After God completed His work, He rested on the seventh day. He certainly did not rest because He was worn out from six straight days of creating. He rested to model rhythm and its importance for us. Isn't it interesting that a year is marked by the revolution around the sun, a month is tied to the phases of the moon, a day is based on the rotation of Earth, and yet there is no cosmic anchor to the week? The week simply exists because God established it as the rhythm in which we would live. He commanded His people to honor the Sabbath as holy, which literally means "set apart." One day each week was set apart to enjoy God and each other as they feasted together on God's good gifts to His people.

This. Is. Awesome!

Yet so few people experience this incredible gift from God. Just like Adam and Eve, we continue to look away from God's offer of life and freedom to take control of and provide for ourselves. Most of us struggle to find our identity in what we do and tend to overdo and overreach to gain more. But isn't it interesting that in our pursuit to be rich in things, we become time-poor? We lose the ability to enjoy time with God and others because we live under the always-on and so-much-to-be-done reality. But when we stop and experience the ceasing and celebrate the Sabbath, we find purpose and meaning for all we do the other days of the week. The Sabbath was given with four primary goals.

1. Remember God's Salvation

   The practice of the Sabbath for the Israelites was directly tied to their freedom from slavery in Egypt. Each Sabbath they remembered their deliverance and praised God that they were a nation set apart for His glory. The Sabbath affords an opportunity to remember that we were saved, we're being saved, and we will be saved. We were saved in the reality of justification, standing righteous before God because of Jesus's sacrifice to free us from the separation of sin. We are being saved as God continues His work of making us more like He created us to live in character and purpose. We will be saved ultimately as Christ returns and God invites His people into an eternal Sabbath rest in His presence. When we remember the fullness of God's salvation, it changes our striving and self-reliance. Instead of complaining and arguing about all that is wrong, we move toward gratitude and humility for the good in our lives. That incites praise in our hearts as we join David through Psalm 51 in the restoration of the joy of salvation.

2. Trust in God's Provision

The Sabbath was experienced as a regular reminder for the Israelites of their time wandering in the wilderness. God literally created new food called manna every day for His people. He provided a double portion on Friday to cover the Sabbath on Saturday. They had all they needed every day as they trusted God, but if they tried to store up extra any other day, it rotted. There was not a clearer picture of God as provider than this. Do you trust that He is able to provide for you? We rest from work for a day to say, "God, You are our provider. You give and take away for a greater purpose than we can see. All we have is from You and for You." The Sabbath serves as a weekly test of faith in order for families to renew their trust in God's provision as enough.

3. Rest for Our Good

We have a tendency to think being made in God's image means we are infinite like God. We think we can push our bodies to function without sleep and rest. It doesn't affect me, you say. I can do this. You may think your normal quick-tempered, tired, and hopped-up-on-caffeine reality is fine, but is it? Is the rested you a better you? Is your rested family a more peaceful family? We don't recognize it until we finally slow down at some point through a vacation or as a result of an injury, and then whoa! We're clear-headed. We can think about something other than work. Around day two you start to notice your family, creation, and the beauty around you again. In a regular rhythm of Sabbath, it's not just life outside that slows down but something inside that calms and cools off a bit. Then you are enabled to draw near to God and allow others in. It is good for you to rest and enjoy what God has given. Don't let guilt or pressure to accomplish more rob you of receiving this weekly gift.

4. Look Forward to Eternal Rest

Ultimately, the Sabbath reminds us that life may be difficult now, but there is freedom coming. Our striving, our working for approval, the curse associated with work (work itself is a gift of God to join with Him in His work), our battle with sin, and our broken bodies will be traded in for sharing in the Father's presence and rest for eternity to come. He invites us to join Him in an eternal rest from sin and its effects on us.

The following illustrations help display the differing experiences of work and rest produced in us as we practice the Sabbath or fall into the natural cycle of the culture around us.

Diagram 1 – Ministry and Work

In the Sabbath cycle, God gives us work as well as rest. They are not aspirations to be achieved but gifts to be received. Both are meant to be enjoyed as participating in and trusting in God's work. As we practice the Sabbath, we intentionally renew and increase our trust in God's provision of work and rest.

Diagram 2 – Natural Cycle

In the natural cycle of our culture, we give our lives to endless productivity and driven achievement. In our exhaustion from work, we seek mind-numbing escape that doesn't prove to be truly restful. We grow in this cycle of anxiety as work demands more and we increasingly desire rest.

We are meant to receive work and rest as gifts from God, knowing everything is from Him and for Him. Escape looks different than enjoyment. Enjoyment receives God's good gifts with gratitude, while escape seeks an avenue to stop feeling or thinking. Escape continues to beckon for more as it never satisfies and only increases the desire for detachment. Lasting joy and peace are found in this beautiful cycle of trust and enjoyment that God gave as a regular practice called the Sabbath.

To begin the practice of the Sabbath, it is important to craft a day of rest that makes sense for your family. There are various theological and practical reasons that cause some to practice 24 hours of rest starting on Friday night through Saturday. Others begin Saturday night through Sunday, and still others practice the Sabbath on the complete day of Sunday. Instead of diving into the differing positions on this, it's more important to encourage the freedom we have in Christ. Paul speaks to this issue as he discusses the law of liberty in his letter to the church at Rome.

> *One person considers one day more sacred than another; another considers every day alike. Each of them should be fully convinced in their own mind. Whoever regards one day as special does so to the Lord. Whoever eats meat does so to the Lord, for they gives thanks to God; and whoever abstains does so to the Lord and gives thanks to God.*

> —Rom. 14:5-6

Instead of debating specifics, we encourage you to craft a day set apart for your family to rest and remember or, otherwise stated, to cease and celebrate. We encourage thoughtful preparation because it takes time to learn what brings rest to your body and rejuvenation to your soul. Use these questions to help guide you to a meaningful and truly restful Sabbath experience.

- What sparks enjoyment of God in our family?
- What sparks enjoyment of each other in our family?
- What brings rest and enjoyment to each person in our family?
- What does our family need to cease or stop doing to set this day apart?
- What would make this our favorite day of the week?
- What time will the Sabbath begin and end for us?

As you process the values and priorities of your family rhythm and weekly Sabbath experience, reflect on Psalm 95.

> *Come, let us sing for joy to the LORD;*
>   *let us shout aloud to the Rock of our salvation.*
> *Let us come before him with thanksgiving*
>   *and extol him with music and song.*
> *For the LORD is the great God,*
>   *the great King above all gods.*
> *In his hand are the depths of the earth,*
>   *and the mountain peaks belong to him.*
> *The sea is his, for he made it,*
>   *and his hands formed the dry land.*
> *Come, let us bow down in worship,*
>   *let us kneel before the LORD our Maker;*
> *for he is our God*
>   *and we are the people of his pasture,*
>   *the flock under his care.*

—Ps. 95:1-7

CHAPTER 4

Table

Gathering

THE TABLE IS one of the most powerful and yet overlooked fundamentals of family. The core metaphor is astonishing when you take time to unpack the depth of meaning and importance the table plays in our lives. The results of consistent gatherings at the family table are vast in depth and breadth of impact. Building your family rhythms around frequent intentional time together at the table will nourish relationships and generational impact beyond any other practice. This regular, multi-sensory experience has the power to not only impact health physically and relationally but to replenish the souls of each person seated at the table. Nothing will activate your family team quite like the table.

Most of our favorite memories in life happen around a table of celebration. They're celebrations of everything from good grades to a work bonus, a birthday, or a wedding that took months of preparation. Almost every traditional, religious, or holiday celebration revolves around a feast of joyful gratitude for God's provision. Certain dishes or desserts can transport you to a specific time and place of memory and delight. Think about some of the top meals you have ever experienced with your family. Can you still see everyone seated around the table and taste the delightful reality of that moment? Isn't it amazing that you were designed with taste buds to enjoy incredible flavor combinations? So many memories flood my mind with Momma's big breakfast, Thanksgiving feasts, Christmas crepes, flying pancakes, birthday parties, candlelight conversations, and more. The food is memorable, but as I reflect, I feel a greater gratitude for who is gathered around the table than what is presented on it.

However, the family table has a tendency to be messy as well. Family meals bring memories of a mingled reality of life and joy as well as struggles and frustration. Your childhood family table may have been an enjoyable source of family connection or a frequent reminder of present brokenness. Or the lack of time at the table together may have reflected the diminished priority of family relationships. Gathering has a way of bringing out the reality of our family—the good, the bad, and the really messy. Yet the table invites us to return to process our lives and continue on our journey. Our McKee family table regularly includes laughter, complaints, correction, stories, questions, spills, sharing, arguing, running around, prayer, tears, and oh yeah, eating too. Regardless of your starting point, you can begin to prioritize the table in your home and develop a life-giving routine of nourishment. First, let's explore the metaphor and then observe the transformational benefits from this key fundamental.

Metaphor

Envision a common family experience of dinner on a weeknight after everyone has been at school or work. Take time to imagine the sights, sounds, smells, touches, and tastes as we explore the environment of the family table. Include one of your favorite family meals as you think through this important metaphor. There may be even more aspects to your family experience to add in order to feel the weight of impact that is possible through your family table.

Everyone feels a need, a weakness, or a desire for something to satisfy a longing in their bodies. This longing motivates activity of preparation that includes selecting, cutting, mixing, heating, seasoning, and cooking dishes for shared enjoyment. Anticipation builds as desire increases due to the delightful scents and the growing hunger of each member of the family. As the time of dining draws near, everyone begins to help with preparations by pouring drinks, gathering silverware, washing hands, and clearing the table. As recipes reach optimal temperature and seasoning, they are transferred to the table. Each person takes their seat as anticipation peaks to satisfy their growing desires.

Portions are given out based on need and regular rationing. A prayer of gratitude for provision and thanks for sacrificial preparation is given. Everyone begins to satisfy their hunger and cravings in their unique patterns of eating and drinking. Careful reminders are given to avoid excess mess or poor etiquette. As hunger and thirsts are quenched, conversations increase with stories from each individual's experience of the day. Sharing, listening, and learning fill the environment with acceptance and belonging. The offering of dessert brings flashes of excitement and joy to remain at the table a while longer.

Delightful enjoyment fills the remaining time together before the work of cleanup begins. Everyone does their part to carry plates, clean the table, wash dishes, and restore order to the home. For a moment, cravings are satisfied, but hunger and longing to return to the table grow over time.

What stood out to you as you read this description of the table experience? What aspect of the table have you been overlooking? How can your family team be developed through an intentional table experience?

Having a seat at the table is foundational for identity and belonging. The desires discussed in the first chapter of being fully known and fully loved are regularly accessible here. In our humanity we come with a fragile dependency to quench our thirsts and satisfy our hunger. We recognize the physical aspects but often overlook the relational, emotional, and spiritual significance of our gatherings. Productivity halts, masks are removed, and we vulnerably share our lives with others who accept us as we are. Whether you're celebrating success or struggling with failure, there is still a seat at the table for you. A table of relational enjoyment is available as you prioritize this time and build intentionality around your table experience. As you continue to feel the depth of meaning surrounding the table, let's look at the benefits of regular family meals.

Benefits

Several studies have been conducted around the impact of family mealtimes. The American College of Pediatricians released a study in May 2014 encouraging physicians to remind families of the importance of the family table. Here's what they wrote:

There are proven benefits to every member when mealtime is a family affair. Families today, however, are less likely to gather at meal times than in the past. Given the protective factors that are conveyed to children and adolescents, pediatricians should encourage parents to make every effort to regularly gather around the "Family Table" for meals.[8]

One of the most protective, developmental, and instructive practices of life is gathering around the table for regular family meals. The study cites the important investments of communication, listening, traditions, meaning, security, and ability to monitor emotional, social, and behavioral development. The ability to observe parents as they process life's challenges regularly enables children to see how adults interact and cooperate. An increase in family meals reveals a simultaneous increase in grades, literacy, language development, and nutrition. It also is preventative in many of the risk areas for adolescents. Children are significantly less likely to engage in eating disorders, screen-time addictions, and depression. Alcohol and drug abuse declines drastically along with emotional and behavioral problems. There is also a notable decrease in sexual activity and teen pregnancy simply from gathering intentionally around the table. Why? Because more family conversation occurs during mealtime than in any other activity.

Simply put, the table brings nourishment physically, mentally, emotionally, relationally, and spiritually. Routine gathering to eat meals together as a family has the potential to change the course of generational legacy in each of these areas. The effects are well-documented for the next generation, but the benefits for parents and grandparents abound. More than 75 percent of families view family dinners as the most important way they connect as a family. Parents feel closer to their kids, and more than 71 percent say they feel more appreciated by their kids when they take time to eat together. About 60 percent of kids say their parents are more relaxed, less stressed, and more fun to be around when they eat together. When generations regularly gather for meals, grandparents have a greater sense of gratitude and hope for passing on the family heritage. The table draws all ages together with opportunities to remember the importance of the name they carry and their place in the greater family narrative.

It is not surprising that Jesus utilized the table as a means of passing on the importance of His sacrifice for His followers. Broken bread and the cup were instituted as constant reminders of freedom and identity as His followers. The invitation of heaven looks less like floating on clouds and more like a family feast of continual enjoyment. The Father invites us to enjoy now and in His presence forever around a table of acceptance, belonging, affirmation, and love.

Conversation

As we've just seen, more family conversation happens during mealtimes than any other activity in the home. This may be one of the first and most important paradigms to shift in your thinking. As we share the table together, we share so much more than food. Life itself is being passed and processed around the table. Your table will grow in greater importance and intentionality as you process these key paradigms.

Family > Google

In 2011, the average American took in five times more information every day than they did in 1986. The amount of information consumed would compare to sitting down and reading 174 newspapers in their entirety each day.[9] Since then, there has been an ever-increasing attempt by marketing and social media to capture the attention of individuals through an explosion of information and images. Many parents feel like they have been replaced as a source of information or learning. It is true that the Internet contains an incomparable amount of information, but the family is uniquely positioned to sit as a filter to process the millions of messages aimed at our brains. The next generation needs wisdom to know what is true and false, and what is a gimmick engineered to waste valuable time. Without this filter, they will fall in line with someone else's agenda and direction for their lives. The majority of messages are simply commercials attempting to gain the consumer's time and money, but others are more sinister in nature with a desire to dictate and control the direction of your life.

The table is the key gathering place to process the day and its messages. Most importantly, you have the opportunity around the table to remove external voices and put away the digital distractions. Turn off screens or turn in phones to emphasize the importance of this valuable family practice. Utilize this time to affirm truth, encourage strengths, and expose lies. It's easy to overlook the power of affirming truth, yet it is vital to bring clarity in order to build a filter for the false through a better understanding of the genuine. The next generation only possesses knowledge of what they have been taught and trained in. It cannot be assumed that the foundations of truth are grounded in their hearts. A subtle lie the next generation believes due to the abundance of images and videos they consume is that they don't measure up. Their lives aren't as important and their strengths aren't as valuable as the "famous" people they view.

You have opportunity in a regular gathering to speak life and encouragement into their hearts. Helping everyone around the table discover their strengths and unique God design to carry forward the family mission is an ongoing process. Finally, we must expose the lies that are being planted in our minds each day. A lie only has power if it is believed to be true. Colossians 2:8 reminds us to be careful "that no one takes you captive through hollow and deceptive philosophy." Remember, the battleground for the heart begins in the mind. Right belief leads to right living and determines the course of your life. The alternative is true as well. Make the most of every opportunity at the table to process surrounding messages and mindsets. Your family is a better source than the endless abyss of opposing ideas and definitions produced online.

Questions > Answers

The table is a place to process life. As we explored in the first fundamental of team, the natural tendency of parents is to drift into the chaperone role. The goal is to make sure kids are fed and in bed safely so you can return to work, practice, or entertainment. Since there is so much work in preparing and cleaning up from a meal, shouldn't it demand some time to linger at the table? One of the best descriptions of Jesus that is repeated multiple times in the Gospels is one who reclined at the table. This image of enjoyment of relationship and sharing life together should mark our tables as well.

It's natural to struggle to think of Jesus listening and enjoying time with others. The image most people have of Him is preaching and teaching at all times. Yet He reclined at tables with His disciples and travel companions to share life together. Have you experienced conversations where time just seemed to fade and nothing else mattered except for being fully present in that moment? Everyone has a seat at the table where they can bring their thoughts and perspectives when we utilize great questions to develop these environments. Don't feel pressure to prepare sermons and rehearsed responses to guide your family to meaningful moments. You can set the table for great discussions with intentional questions. Great questions have the power to transform any environment from meaningless to memorable. Questions create curiosity. Curiosity leads to discovery and exploration of our perspectives and passions. Questions bring opportunity to reveal what is stirring in our hearts. As you ask open-ended questions, pay close attention to responses. "The purposes of a person's heart are deep waters, but one who has insight draws them out" (Prov. 20:5).

Everyone Shares

Great questions develop environments of opportunity for everyone to share their perspectives and experiences. Pay attention to what is shared and how it is communicated. Open conversation at the table reveals the emotional and relational climate of each person's life and the family as a whole. However, families are usually comprised of over-talkers and internal processors. Thriving conversational environments are only achieved when the energy of sharing is passed around the circle.

In order to develop this thriving environment, it is important to develop ground rules to guide your table. A simple guiding statement might be, "At our table everyone shares, and everyone cares." This reminds the over-talkers to limit their desire for detailed storytelling and encourages the internal processors to honor everyone with their engagement. Emphasize care by asking reflective questions as someone else shares their thoughts. This practice has the potential to validate those sharing and develop social listening skills in others. It also will require someone to facilitate and keep the conversation moving around the table and away from arguments and invalidation.

The questions you choose to guide these environments should be easy to respond to with the potential for greater depth. Question categories that help guide everyone to share include highs and lows, new or different experiences, individual gratitude, specific encouragement, friend profiles, prayer requests, and personal goals. Open and approachable questions can lead to life-giving conversations. Your family may benefit through repetition of questions or the spontaneity of new conversation starters. Regardless of the method, it is important to encourage lingering at the table in order to value relationships over entertainment and productivity.

Everyone Serves

One of the most powerful examples of humility in the history of humanity happened at a table.

> *Jesus knew that the Father had put all things under his power, and that he had come from God and was returning to God; so he got up from the meal, took off his outer clothing, and wrapped a towel around his waist. After that, he poured water into a basin and began to wash his disciples' feet, drying them with the towel that was wrapped around him.*
>
> —John 13:3-5

Jesus used His position of authority to serve instead of being served (Matt. 20:28). Deserving of the most important seat at the table, Jesus took the lowest place of a servant to wash the disciples' feet. After washing, He encouraged the disciples to do for others as He had done for them. Following the way of Jesus is marked with continual growth in humility through serving. The table offers a daily opportunity to activate the value of serving one another humbly in love (Gal. 5:13) for every person in your family.

Although most families have one person who is more gifted in preparing meals, the table presents several roles of service that any age can engage in. Setting the table, gathering drinks, cooking, washing dishes, and cleaning up can either exhaust individuals or activate a family team in service. It's not simply about food. It's about the process of creating together and the conversations that happen while chopping a salad. It's the process of passing on knowledge, character, and skills from one generation to the next. A rule in our house is that no one is seated until everyone is seated. This simple principle encourages everyone to fulfill a role of helping the family get the meal on the table to enable an experience of dinner together. Without this principle, the preparer of the meal can often feel like a waiter or waitress meeting the demands of the customers. After sharing the meal, serving skills are developed by encouraging cleanup and dishes. You can either build a rotation of dish duties or create an expectation of finishing together before moving to other activities.

If you're in the habit of doing everything for your children or others at the table, your servant heart is appreciated. However, you are probably wearing yourself out and accidentally crippling others into selfish practices. One of the reasons your role is easily taken for granted is that others haven't experienced the challenge of doing it themselves. Taking the servant role is a value to be shared among the family, not simply for one member of the family to fulfill for the others. Everyone needs to feel needed and given opportunities to meet the needs of others in age-appropriate ways. When everyone serves, the family team is encouraged to live out the character of Christ's humility and empowered to take responsibility for their roles on the team.

Anchor

The Sabbath meal is the most important regular table practice to transform your family team. This meal anchors the Sabbath experience as a dividing line between normal life and sacred rest. Without a clear beginning or ending, it will be tempting to let regular responsibilities creep into this sacred time. Setting the Sabbath apart to cease, connect, and celebrate as a regular rhythm for your family will develop margin, increase enjoyment, normalize depth, and reinforce identity. Some families utilize the meal as the ending of a great Sabbath experience or a kickoff to rest and enjoyment.

For Jewish families who observe Shabbat, there are three meals, but the first is the most significant. Since Shabbat begins on Friday at sundown and ends on Saturday at nightfall, the first meal begins on Friday night. The Shabbat tables are elegantly set, and families often sing traditional songs, engage in meaningful conversation, and speak blessings over the family. Traditional food, practices, and decor bring distinction to the meal as it also brings distinction to the family identity. As the meal is set apart from normal life, so the family is set apart for a divine purpose.

As stated in the previous chapter on time, your family doesn't have to be Jewish or part of a ritualistic tribe to experience the blessing of the Sabbath. Jesus reminds us that God established the Sabbath "for man, not man for the Sabbath" (Mark 2:27).

Building the Sabbath meal into your rhythm will demand a shift in your family and enable you to truly cease, connect, and celebrate in a weekly routine. You will need to craft a meal experience that works for the unique stage of family life you are in, but it should also include the elements you hope to repeat for years and even generations to come. Don't feel pressure to establish a perfect experience, but include elements that set this meal apart from your daily gatherings. As you begin this family custom, we encourage you to start with a lot of grace, knowing that this is a change for your family. It will not be a picture-perfect practice from the beginning, but you will improve with each celebration. Remember, the table may be messy, but it nourishes us physically, spiritually, relationally, and emotionally.

Set Apart

Decor and candles assist in distinguishing this meal from others. As my family began our Sabbath meal experience, we wanted to reinforce our family name and improve the table environment to reflect its importance. We bought chargers (decorative plates) and decided to use our nicer tableware. As we finished preparing the food, we invited our children to decorate the table and set the environment for our Sabbath meal. We learned that scents are strongly linked to memory and emotion. Breathing in a fragrance takes a direct route to the limbic system, which impacts the regions of the brain related to emotion and memory. As a reflection of our family name, we purchased two fireside candles. We began the meal by lighting one candle to represent ceasing and the other to emphasize celebrating. Before prayer, we recited our family mission and the meaning of our name together through questions and responses. After the meal, we took time to read Scripture and discuss some aspect of faith formation. Think through your Sabbath meal experience by using these questions:

- What decorations would set this meal apart from others?
- What candles, fragrance, or reminders would represent our family name?
- How can everyone join in to prepare for or clean up the meal?
- What resource could help guide us as we build up our family in faith?

Celebrate

Who doesn't love to celebrate? Life is filled with reasons to celebrate and share joy as a family. Add age-appropriate fun to your family gathering to help everyone look forward to this experience. The Sabbath isn't a ritual to endure but a weekly gift to enjoy. We don't drink carbonated beverages very often in our family, but at our Sabbath meal, everyone gets to choose their bubbly drink. Music before and after the meal may help create environments of dancing and singing that add a sweet sprinkling of joy to the table. Knowing your family and their pathways of enjoyment will help everyone anticipate the arrival of the Sabbath.

This is a weekly opportunity to celebrate God's faithfulness and goodness to your family. In our culture of complaining and arguing, thanksgiving and encouragement serve as great medicine for our souls. Each week offers the opportunity to look back to recognize God's faithfulness in the past, acknowledge His presence in the moment, and trust Him for continued leadership in the future. There is truly so much to celebrate when we take time to process. Scripture is filled with encouragements and commands to give thanks, praise, worship, dance, shout, and sing whether in the desert or a fortified city. "Taste and see that the LORD is good; blessed is the one who takes refuge in him" (Ps. 34:8). This practice will anchor your faith in God's presence and your ability to guide your family forward into the mission God has set out for you. Think through your family pathways to celebration using these questions:

- What would encourage an environment of celebration as we prepare for the meal?
- What aspect of our meal or decor will signify celebration?
- What questions or conversations motivate gratitude in our family?

Blessing

A blessing is defined as God's favor and protection. We have the opportunity to pass this blessing on to our children as we close out the meal. Affirming our child's identity as part of our family and God's gifting in them individually will build confidence to carry the family mission forward.

The practice of blessing builds opportunity in which the people involved remember and acknowledge their true nature and worth. One strengthens another with a reminder of shalom or wholeness found in the Father and in their family identity. The parent giving the blessing is often encouraged as much as the receiver. Some parents speak written or memorized prayers over their children, and others change their prayer to fit that week's focus or specific needs in their child. Again, this is based on your family stage and situation. Craft a blessing experience where you are able to speak life and favor over your children to remind them of God's love and affirmation for them, as well as your own. Process ahead of time how you want to set up this environment of blessing.

- Who will speak a blessing over whom?
- What qualities or attributes do you want to emphasize in this blessing?
- What scripture or biblical character might add depth to our words?
- When will we practice this time of blessing—at the end of the meal or at the end of teaching or conversation?

Allow this blessing to guide you as you prepare to set the table of Sabbath blessing.

> *Blessed are all who fear the LORD,*
>   *who walk in obedience to him.*
> *You will eat the fruit of your labor;*
>   *blessings and prosperity will be yours.*
> *Your wife will be like a fruitful vine*
>   *within your house;*
> *your children will be like olive shoots*
>   *around your table.*
> *Yes, this will be the blessing*
>   *for the man who fears the LORD.*
> *May the LORD bless you from Zion;*
>   *may you see the prosperity of Jerusalem*
>   *all the days of your life.*
> *May you live to see your children's children—*
>   *peace be on Israel.*

—Ps. 128

CHAPTER 5

Tech

Tool

OW DOES TECHNOLOGY find its way into the fundamentals of family? How can it be in the same category as the other timeless fundamentals? First of all, technology has made its way into every corner of the home. If you don't have a plan for tech, then tech will have a plan for you. Second, families have always had to find ways to adapt to changing tools, challenges, and inventions. Adapting to innovation is not a new practice, but the speed at which it is changing and the pervasive impact of technology on the family demand a focused plan.

My father has been a construction worker, specifically an electrician, throughout most of his life. He can build pretty much anything, which inspires the grandkids to say, "God made Papaw, and Papaw made everything else." Every time he approaches a new project, he agrees with my mom to do the work if he can buy a new tool. The right tool will drastically increase his ability to complete the project. Alongside my dad,

I have grown increasingly fascinated with tools throughout my lifetime.

Early in life, I was given a small hammer to "help" work on projects. As a preteen, I was invited to use larger tools to help chop and split wood for winter. As I grew in strength, I was invited to be a "gopher" at the job sites. I was told to "go for" the tools and supplies others needed. Often I created more work than help as I curiously messed up tool after tool. Dad was often heard saying, "Boy, you would tear up an iron wedge."

During my teenage years, I found myself wiring houses alongside my dad. I learned that I needed the right drill or drill bit to make holes for the wire in specific places or materials. After a ton of mistakes and frequent correction, I gained access to more tools as I was entrusted with more responsibility on the jobs. Now I enjoy building and remodeling with my own increasing supply of tools. I have the privilege and daunting responsibility to train my kids through the same process of responsibility and freedom.

Technology is an amoral tool. That means technology itself is neither good nor evil. As technology increases, it simply speeds up the opportunity for the good or evil found in the heart of the user. Just as I was entrusted with tools in a graduated process, so our homes should have a process of increasing freedoms alongside an increase in responsibility with technology. Most families don't have a plan or process for technology except for trying to hold off purchasing it as long as possible and scolding others for spending too much time on screens. As we advance in technology and increase freedom in our home, we must assess the potential gains and losses that come with each transition and device.

Tech Gains and Losses

There are some who believe that all technology is evil and point to the bite-out-of-the-apple logo as proof of its satanic origin. It is true that the iPhone brought drastic changes to our daily interactions with technology, but it would be impossible to characterize every activity on it as evil. The iPhone simply moved the opportunity for good and evil into our pockets and increased the speed of opportunity with each new generation. However, technology reaches a vast spectrum from the sundial and light bulb to the smartwatch and space station. Each advancement should be evaluated before adding it to our lives and homes. Interestingly, we can take a lesson from the Amish on this process. As the elder patriarchs assessed the automobile as a potential new technology for their community, they recognized the benefits for work and business. However, one factor led them to ultimately dismiss the addition of cars and trucks. Speedy and convenient transportation at their fingertips would lead to spending more time away from family, home, and the community.

I'm not attempting to usher in a horse and buggy revolution, but I believe there is a powerful lesson in the Amish assessment. They recognized the potential gains of embracing an emerging technology but also assessed the concerns for their community values. Each advancement in tech usually comes with greater opportunities, speed, ease, and flexibility. New opportunities to travel, explore, create, and discover accompany every invention and innovation. Speed and ease increase through changes from candles to LEDs, snail mail to e-mail, maps to GPS, and landlines to smartphones, just to name a few. Can you imagine going back to candles or paper maps? Finally, the flexibility gained through technology is a blessing and a curse. The blessing of portable devices is that we are able to work from anywhere, and the curse is the same. We are able to work from anywhere.

Understanding the blessing and the challenge associated with each advancement is vital to wise engagement and utilization. Much has inarguably been gained, but significant losses accompany these changes to everyday life. Alongside the previously mentioned gains are the consistent cultural losses of focus, relationships, literacy, honor, and meaning. Continuous partial attention is our new normal as focused attention spans have significantly decreased.[10] We mistake being busy and stressed for doing important work while much of our time is spent dealing with the flood of attempts to gain our attention. With our attention goes our time, and time with technology is pulled from the same pie as people. Relational intimacy and depth have seen a significant decline through increased use of technology. There is a usual gain in breadth of shallow relationships but at the cost of depth in close personal relationships.

It's interesting that advancement in technology often makes us feel superior in intelligence to the previous generation. Yet the alternative is often true. Take, for instance, memorizing friends' phone numbers, for those who remember this practice. I used to know all my friends' phone numbers in rapid recall, but now, since my phone retains all this information for me, I don't even know my mom's number by heart. Did this advancement make me smarter or dumber? Literacy has witnessed a remarkable decline in reading levels as adults peruse quick news articles with simplistic language to increase clicks and children spend less focused time in books and vocabulary development. Grappling with theological and philosophical depth is abandoned in pursuit of the quick and fleeting digital distractions.

In addition to the losses of focus, relationships, and literacy, there is a continual diminishing of honor and meaning. Honor and integrity refer to strength in the highest moral principles and the absence of deceit or fraud. It is achieved through consistent perseverance in refusing temptation, devoted study, and intentionality in growth of character. The root Hebrew word is *kabod*, which means "heavy or weighty." We are meant to grow in depth of meaning and purpose personally and give weight or meaning to those around us as well. Instead, honor and meaning are often reduced in priority behind opportunity and privacy. Technology advancements have increased a two-way digital door that not only gives opportunity to the user but also constant potential for programmers to gain and keep our attention. Our attention shapes our hearts and minds. Solomon cautions in his vast wisdom, "Above all else, guard your heart, for everything you do flows from it" (Prov. 4:23).

To guard and guide the hearts of those who carry our family name, we must have a plan for how we will assess and utilize technology in our homes. Your time spent proactively planning will prevent your endless reactive battles of catching up to the advancing speed and influence of technology in your home.

Purpose

Adults tend to assess the addition of a new technology to the home based on its purpose and potential benefit for the family. They normally ask, "What will this do for me or us?" If a new technology fits within the budget and simplifies a task or adds meaning or purpose to the family, people will purchase it. However, children ask a different question based on their curiosity. They simply ask, "What will this do?" They will play with and explore all the functionality of a device as a source of fun and discovery. These inherent differences in approach, among several other factors, lead to the primary difficulties in managing the use of technology in the home.

Pragmatism and creativity both retain merit in utilization. Parents have the opportunity to model and teach purpose in their practice and process of adding devices to the home. Do not buy more devices for the home simply because they're new or because someone wants them. We must assess the benefits and challenges before we move forward with purchases or request gifts. If the primary gain is an extra distraction or additional digital pacifier, then we should explore other routes. Walk through your additional technology analysis with your children to understand the why behind your decision. Parents must assess purpose in adding and model purpose in utilization. Your children are unable to see what you are doing on a personal device and often assume you are using it as they would. At times it is beneficial to speak out loud what you are accomplishing or why you put your phone out of reach at times. While it is important to model and assess purpose, parents must also learn to ask curious questions in order to understand the pathways children will choose when using technology.

Technology is not evil, but it has the potential to speed up the opportunity to lose many other meaningful aspects of life. As you build a plan for tech in your home, use the following TECH acrostic to guide your conversations. It will be beneficial to purchase or implement a tool that will allow you to remain in open accountability through preset controls and filters to guide regular usage.

T – Time Limits

According to the Environmental Protection Agency, the average American spends 93 percent of their time indoors and in vehicles. Only 7 percent of modern Americans' time is currently spent outdoors, and this number continues to decrease as technology usage increases.[11] Creativity, exercise, and exploration naturally happen in outdoor environments and benefit the development of parents and children alike.

Linking child obesity, low attention spans, and long-term health issues to this lack of outdoor activity, the National Recreation and Park Association stated, "Children today spend less time outdoors than any other generation, devoting only four to seven minutes to unstructured outdoor play per day while spending an average of seven and a half hours in front of electronic media."[12] Seven minutes versus seven hours—wow! Why have we allowed this massive shift in time utilization for the next generation? Prepare for conviction; it's easier. Pragmatically it's easier to keep accomplishing tasks and work if our children are sedentary. It feels safer to let them consume digital media inside than allowing and encourage them to get outside and build muscles and play creatively. Parents are often worried about physical harm and expectations of supervision. Parents do not want to be pulled away from the tasks they hope to accomplish or media they desire to consume. That brings us to the first key truth: we all need time limits.

There is a war for your family's attention, and you are probably losing the battle to others' intentions for you. Everything you have ever done online is recorded, algorithmically sorted, and systematically deployed to regain your focus and retain your time. While most of this is financially motivated, there are also political, social, religious, and emotional drivers at play. Simply scrolling through any media feed will undoubtedly contain additional links, advertisements, or assistance by auto-playing the next video in the stream.

The Social Dilemma, a documentary released in 2020, questions the ethics of mental manipulation as tech experts expose the inherent dangers of using their digital platforms.[13] Look at these two notable quotes from the documentary:

If you are not paying for the product, then you are the product.

It's the gradual, slight, imperceptible change in your own behavior and perception that is the product.[14]

If supercomputers are pointed at the brains of our children with a desire to change their behaviors and perceptions, is this sedentary option safer? The potential physical dangers of outside play pale compared to the potential manipulative shift of worldview and motivation that is vying for the hearts and minds of the next generation. It is vital for the family to set screen times and predetermined time limits to break compulsive or addictive behaviors that accompany digital consumption.

Parents must also wrestle with their personal attention and the time they spend on devices. Digital discipleship is caught more than it is taught. We must avoid our tendency to see children as a distraction from more important work. In a multigenerational vision, we recognize that our children are the most important work to extend a lasting legacy.

One notable danger of smartphones and personal devices is that they enable work responsibilities to creep into every moment in and away from the office. As stated earlier, it is a blessing and a curse to be able to work from anywhere. Keeping a multigenerational team view of family in mind will guide you to make the most of your time together as a family. Curating a predetermined list of desired shows, videos, and games will develop intentionality behind your media use. Build safeguards to help resist the temptation to scroll and mindlessly search for something in order to escape reality.

Most tech devices come with parental controls, or you can purchase a subscription or companion device to manage screen time and filter which websites your kids can visit. Many even offer specific app or category limits to distinguish between productive and entertainment utilization. An external digital solution is necessary to keep you from setting multiple timers and regularly having to chase children off of screens. We must face the reality that it is almost impossible to keep track of the amount of digital consumption on our own in modern culture. We need help. Simplify the process by developing time limits and digital bedtimes for each person in your home. Invite your children into this process, and develop intentional agreement to ease future conversations when limits are reached. Even if you decide to add more time on a specific day, reaching a time limit will trigger a conversation on purpose and the utilization of focus. Remember, in family life, we spell love T-I-M-E.

E – Eliminate Secrecy

After developing intentional time limits for each person based on age and life stage, the next step is to eliminate secrecy. The digital doorway is a two-way door with opportunities for the user to accidentally stumble onto dangerous content and for strangers to target the user for their own intentions. Conversations about these dangers are necessary as increased access is given to the next generation. Moving usage to public environments over private spaces is a key prohibiter of digital dangers.

One of the easiest filters to implement in assessing the times and spaces for appropriate online use is the real-life test, which asks, "Would I allow my kid to do this in real, offline life?" Would you allow your child to have a limitless library of movies, magazines, and media in their room alone? Would you allow your child to meet strangers in private rooms without knowing anything about the other person? Is it healthy or developmentally helpful for a child to sit mindlessly in the same spot for hours? The real-life test helps us honestly assess tech usage in ways we naturally overlook in modern culture. Shining a light of accountability on time, content, and relationships is the primary goal of digital parenting.

The average age of initial viewing of Internet pornography is 11 years old. Children aren't always looking for pornography; it is literally programmed to find them. Tweens and teens possess a natural curiosity about sex. If parents are not discussing sex before these questions arise, curiosity will lead them to search the Internet. Do you really want your child googling sex? And as they hear slang thrown around at school, they will be tempted to search, "What is _____?"

Developing an open discussion about topics like sex in your family will reduce wrestling with secrecy and fighting for privacy. Pure Hope Quest parenting curriculum helped guide us to develop this environment with two key commitments with our children. After discussing God's better plan for sex, we promised them that they could ask us anything moving forward. We assured our kids that we would always tell them the truth and that they wouldn't get in trouble for asking. This proactive conversation has kept us from several reactive strategies to attempt to fix the brokenness they might have curiously stumbled upon.

Eliminate secrecy by allowing light and accountability to guide tech engagement with your family. Let light shine in all areas of your home with straightforward boundaries and guardrails to guide time with external media. In our home, screens do not go into bedrooms or private spaces. Phones and personal devices charge in our living room. As parents, we have passwords and open access to check devices at any time for regular accountability. These clear boundaries encourage transparency and prevent many possible negative technology pitfalls. The Apostle John uses the simple yet profound metaphor of light and darkness to lead us. "But if we walk in the light, as he is in the light, we have fellowship with one another, and the blood of Jesus, his Son, purifies us from all sin" (1 John 1:7).

In the light there is no hiding or fighting for privacy. We find fellowship with God and each other as we walk in the light together. If someone in your home is fighting for privacy, it is often but not always an indicator that they are hiding something. Gently and intentionally take steps forward to promote transparency, and prepare to approach secret struggles with grace and truth. We find healing and freedom as we come out of the darkness of shame and embrace the forgiveness Christ offers to overcome guilt, addictions, and failure.

C – Create and Connect

Our first two paradigms to rethink in approaching technology build defensive safeguards for the vast array of potential digital dangers. Now let's move on to an offensive strategy to guide technology use to its greatest purpose in our families. While there are many potentially harmful pitfalls, there are positive uses as well. It is important to cast vision for and motivate toward these uses or there will be a natural move toward nothingness or destructive patterns. A simple way to illustrate the best proactive uses of technology is the following matrix.

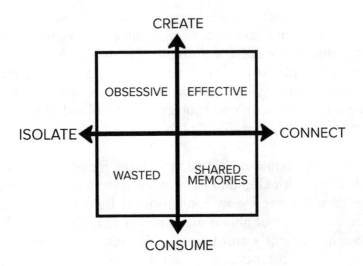

CREATE

OBSESSIVE | EFFECTIVE

ISOLATE ← → CONNECT

WASTED | SHARED MEMORIES

CONSUME

There are two primary spectrums we need to assess together as we approach media. We can employ technology to move us toward creating or consuming. Learning to play instruments, developing skills, preparing recipes, and sharing digital creations help develop abilities and confidence. Creating promotes innovation and imagination that celebrates the originality in your home. Consuming entails passive viewing and unintentional entertainment. Consuming isn't all bad, but very little of it is positively produced, and studies even show it is not even as restful as it is perceived to be. Active rest is often more restorative to the body, mind, and soul through social, physical, and spiritual engagement instead of digital consumption.

Another helpful spectrum to assess in the utilization of technology is relational connection or isolation. Connection should be targeted as an overarching goal for your family and can be achieved through technology as well. Shared experiences are key developers of relationships. Intentionally choosing a show, game, or series to share as a family can deepen family bonds through the development of common quotes and stories to relate to.

Different seasons of the year, such as winters in the northern states, may foster increased connection through media. However, seasons of good weather may benefit through consistent connection outside of media. The opposite end of the relational spectrum and often the most frequent utilization of technology is found in isolation. As with consuming over connection, isolation is not to be totally rejected as some personality style or need for personal time to recharge. However, consuming in isolation for extended periods of time on a regular basis opens the door to digital dangers as well as significant wasting of the valuable opportunities of time.

As stated previously, technology is a tool that simply speeds up the opportunity for good or evil. Consuming in isolation can lead to a significant wasting of time and opportunity and developing destructive lifestyle habits. In its extreme form, creating in isolation leads to an obsessive, self-motivated attitude consumed with perfectionism and image protection. Consuming media while connected with others can develop shared experiences, but without movement toward meaning, it simply leaves users entertained. When utilized for creativity and connection, technology finds its greatest opportunity to advance your family mission. Regardless of where you find your family's current utilization, families will benefit by moving toward a culture of greater connection and creativity.

This can be as simple as developing a regular, meaningful discussion after watching movies together. I usually ask our children, "Since every story gets its power from The Story, how did you see the story of God in that movie?" You can also schedule extended family digital gatherings to develop connection with your greater multigenerational team. The opportunities for connection and creativity are just as endless as the potential for danger and distraction. Be careful to resist legalism and immediate drastic changes as you move your family toward more effective digital engagement. Find unique pathways for your family and stage of life to cast vision toward a more effective use of technology.

H – Honor Always

Honor is another proactive and offensive guide to technology. Through digital doorways we are called to honor God, other people, and our family. Honor, as explored in technology losses, literally means full value or weightiness. To honor is to value a greater good or regard with great respect. To possess honor describes someone of high moral worth or great achievement. Honor is a virtue that beckons us to purity, encouragement, honesty, compassion, and worship. God is the first to be honored with our lives as the one with the highest value and weightiness. In His character we find one worthy of honor, glory, and praise. "Now to the King eternal, immortal, invisible, the only God, be honor and glory for ever and ever. Amen" (1 Tim. 1:17). As His children, we are meant to represent Him well online and offline with our lives. Christians are declared His ambassadors as though God were making His appeal to humanity through us. Honoring God as our primary goal will develop a filter for deciding which media is worth engaging with and a guide for how we relate to others.

One of the most important reminders to keep in constant view when posting or engaging online is that everything shared digitally is potentially public forever. As our lives integrate more with personal devices, our offline lives will as well. Conversations, images, and videos shared online should be honorable because they can and will be used to develop a digital profile of you as a person. Honoring God with posts and Internet history honors your future self with a strong record of high moral character. One thoughtless or shortsighted post has cost many people their careers and potential positions of influence.

Honoring other people online encourages them to live out God's specific calling for their lives. Noticing the good in others and giving specific encouragement is a life-giving practice. Here is a simple principle to guide your replies and comments online: praise in public, correct in private. Taking time to encourage speaks value to the recipient, brings life to others who view your comment, and rejects any jealousy that might attempt to take root in your heart. We are encouraged by Paul to "be devoted to one another in love. Honor one another above yourselves" (Rom. 12:10).

The opposite practice is true as well. Negativity breeds negativity toward the recipient, readers, and yourself. The real-life test reminds us that we wouldn't yell our disagreements with others at the top of our lungs in the middle of the mall. Yet that is how many people respond online with critical and damaging comments. If there is an issue of disagreement or correction that needs to be dealt with, it is better to approach it in private on a personal level. There is so much to be celebrated as we join God's restorative process and replace shame with dignity and value through honoring others.

Finally, individuals must remember that they don't post or view only for themselves but also represent their multigenerational team with their individual choices. If Internet histories and seemingly private conversations were all posted in public spaces, what would be the result for your family? Would people be impressed at your family's wise engagement with technology? Or would you be ashamed to show your face in public settings due to activity that has been taking place in "secret" settings? The reality of everything digital being stored on servers somewhere brings this imaginative scenario closer to possibility, especially if one of your family members decides to go into politics. Honoring the family through technology means engaging online with high morality and adding to, not subtracting from, the name that is carried by each person in the family. Honor always stands as a guiding value for all aspects of life, which will prove beneficial as the lines between online and offline progressively blur.

Process

After rethinking our need for time limits, elimination of secrecy, creativity, connection, and honor in utilizing technology, we must implement the practice of a graduated process of freedom and self-regulation. As noted previously, technology is a tool with potential to build or break apart our family experiences. Just as my father didn't hand me a powered nail gun or sledgehammer as a toddler, parents should progressively release access to children based on maturity and trust. This process will guard against the dangers associated with irresponsible, unfiltered access and cast vision for the future goal of unsupervised self-regulation that will hopefully be experienced before children leave the home for college or career.

A guiding principle for this process is that greater responsibility leads to greater freedom.

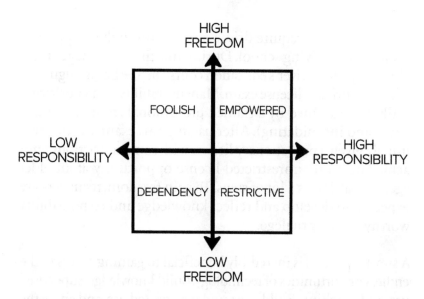

Giving freedom without responsibility inevitably leads to foolish failure. Increasing responsibility and knowledge before increasing freedom will lead to a wiser utilization of that freedom. Just as the greatest protection from drowning is learning to swim, so we must teach our children to use technology well before unleashing them into total digital freedom.

A responsibility level is assessed through regularly meeting age-appropriate and reasonable expectations. As more freedom is given, more responsibility is expected. Think about the process that is legally in place to allow your child to start driving. First, children spend significant time watching you drive and learning from your good—and bad—driving habits. Next, they have to reach a specific age (which varies, depending on the state) to be eligible to take a test and get a permit. Potential drivers normally study a book or manual to prepare for this exam. During the learner's permit period, new drivers are expected to complete a significant number of driving hours under parental supervision and coaching.

Many states also require driver training through an approved professional driving school. During this time, a teenager must also complete a driver's education course before being eligible to take their driver's license exam. Maneuverability and safe driving skills are examined by a trained professional (mine was angry, strict, and intimidating). After passing this exam, the driver is usually given a probationary license with some restrictions until achieving a full, unrestricted license opportunity at an older age. Whoa! That's a lot of steps. To gain freedom, teenagers are expected to develop and reflect knowledge and responsibility worthy of that privilege.

A similar process is incredibly beneficial to gaining access to the endless opportunities of technology. Build knowledge, supervised use, and coaching. Build trust under restricted use, and enjoy the freedom of self-regulated, unrestricted digital engagement. It is so important to cast a vision with children from the beginning that the goal is to move toward self-regulated, unrestricted access, but the process is meant to guard and guide them to arrive at the goal with wisdom and safety. Personal responsibility will be developed through setting clear boundaries and guiding goals. There is potentially greater danger to your child's emotional, mental, spiritual, and relational health from private, unfiltered technology usage than almost any other source in our modern world.

An example from our family experience is best illustrated in our process to give our teenager his first smartphone. First, our desire was to build knowledge and character to prepare him to handle this freedom. He was given a few options of books he would like to read in order to understand the opportunities and dangers of a personal device. He was also given a section of Scripture to memorize to prepare his heart for proper usage. After completing these, we sat down with a tech contract outlining our expectations and his clear commitments. Our contract included our open access to and ownership of his phone, clear boundaries for texting and online engagement, a regular charging location, and encouragements toward future open access. After proving faithful over an extended season with texting and Internet use, we began the discussion about social media use.

To prepare for social media access, we again assigned a book to build knowledge of potential dangers and watched a documentary as a family. Now, with limited parental supervision and regular check-ins regarding his texts and online use, he has grown in responsibility and personal boundaries. We look forward to the day when we are able to empower him with complete self-regulation and trust his wise use of time and personal boundaries to choose content. However, as we maintain a strong connection relationally, we hope to continue to be a source of wisdom and guidance.

The goal for parents must be responsibility, not restrictions. We want to help guide them to freedom just as Paul talks about in his letter to the Galatians. Freedom isn't found simply in the ability to do what you want but in the pursuit of God's best for our lives. Freedom can lead to greater restrictions or greater freedoms based on how it is employed.

> *It is absolutely clear that God has called you to a free life. Just make sure that you don't use this freedom as an excuse to do whatever you want to do and destroy your freedom. Rather, use your freedom to serve one another in love; that's how freedom grows. For everything we know about God's Word is summed up in a single sentence: Love others as you love yourself. That's an act of true freedom.*

> —Gal. 5:13-14 (MSG)

Christ has set us free from the power of sin and death because of His sacrifice on our behalf. This freedom is made possible by the amazing offer of grace instead of personal punishment and eternal restriction. Because of the power of grace, we are not struggling to be free but rather free to struggle. There is a strong probability that your child will stumble through this process and initiate a tightening of restrictions for a season. You should not receive this with anger and wrath but with compassion and guidance toward the goal of freedom and personal responsibility. This is why we stress the importance of an initial agreement with your child. The agreement clearly defines potential losses of freedom and helps lessen the shock of new restrictions or short-term loss of the device.

Knowledge leads to responsibility. Responsibility leads to greater freedom. Freedom yields personal convictions and guiding principles. Empower your child for the end goal with tech and other avenues of freedom. As they responsibly use technology on their own, you will be so glad you took the time to walk this important process together. This process could also apply to gaming devices, personal computers, television, and any device with freedom of access. Use these questions to guide you as you develop a clear plan and process for technology in your home.

- What are realistic time limits for individuals in our home?
- What practices will help eliminate secrecy with technology use?
- How can we move toward a greater environment of creativity and connection? What new practices will enable this? What changes can we make to current practices?
- How can we clarify the vision of honor always in our family?
- What age will we begin allowing our child to have a personal device?

- What resources will we choose to educate our child for responsible tech usage?
- When could we as a family observe a technology fast to encourage a digital detox?
- What needs to be done in our home to restore accountability and reclaim life offline?

Meditate on the wisdom of this psalm as you process your plan for technology in your family.

Blessed is the one
  who does not walk in step with the wicked
or stand in the way that sinners take
  or sit in the company of mockers,
but whose delight is in the law of the Lord,
  and who meditates on his law day and night.
That person is like a tree planted by streams of water,
  which yields its fruit in season
and whose leaf does not wither—
  whatever they do prospers.
Not so the wicked!
  They are like chaff
  that the wind blows away.
Therefore the wicked will not stand in the judgment,
  nor sinners in the assembly of the righteous.
For the Lord *watches over the way of the righteous,*
  but the way of the wicked leads to destruction.

—Ps. 1

6

Traditions

Value

IN OUR SECOND family fundamental we explored time. We emphasized the importance of weekly family rhythms to bring life to our mission and connection as a family. The concept of a metronome helped us evaluate our BPMs, or speed at which our family is paced. As we focus on traditions, let's shift to another music metaphor of crescendos. A crescendo is "a gradual increase in volume of a musical passage."[15] Many songs brilliantly illustrate the use of crescendo, from Beethoven's Symphony No. 5 to the epic guitar solo in Free Bird. These maximum moments are anticipated from the first note of a song and often stand as the most memorable segment. However, everything can't be a crescendo or it would just be a really loud song. We live in an increasingly loud culture that is fighting for our attention, and today it takes something significant to gain our focus. Does everyone in your family know what really matters? The easiest way to understand what is most valued in a family is to recognize what is most celebrated. You celebrate the things you value.

Strong families build family and faith identity through deep and meaningful occasions to party. Does your family celebrate well?

Traditions stand as key crescendo moments for your family to emphasize primary values and mark key milestones on your family journey. The word *tradition* means handing down for safekeeping or transmission of value, belief, or practice from generation to generation. There is actually a legal protection of traditions to preserve the cultural heritage of humankind. The destruction of practices of heritage and cultural memory is considered a part of psychological warfare. Traditions root us into a story greater than our individual lives and link us to an enduring identity that transcends our personal experience.

Moses introduced several traditions to anchor the Israelites in remembrance of God's faithfulness to His people and to emphasize obedience and identity in the present. Apart from the weekly feast of Shabbat, Jewish families were called to observe seven feasts throughout the year, which Moses outlined with clarity in Leviticus 23. Each feast involves a unique practice to encourage remembrance and a sacrifice to develop dependence on God as the source of their identity as a people and the giver of every good blessing. Many of these feasts lasted seven days. God wanted his people to rest and party. What a good God!

As God declared His plan to deliver His people from Egypt (Exod. 12), He already included the future feast to remember this moment well. The depth of meaning found in the blood of a lamb brushed across the doorframes of a home was not meant simply to direct the warrior angel but to link all generations to the promise of a perfect Lamb who would take away the sins of the world. The Passover celebration was instituted to never forget God's deliverance from slavery and to believe in His future deliverance from sin and death through the Messiah.

Remember, these instructions are a permanent law that you and your descendants must observe forever. When you enter the land the LORD has promised to give you, you will continue to observe this ceremony. Then your children will ask, "What does this ceremony mean?"

—Exod. 12:24-26 (NLT)

God knew the next generation would not have experienced His deliverance personally but that experiencing a feast could anchor their faith through symbols and sacrifices. The children would ask, "What does this ceremony mean?"—or more simply, "Why?" Each tradition we observe as a family has the opportunity to solidify our why and our family mission. However, most families in Western culture have allowed holidays and traditions to fall more into the quick and fleeting consumerism category. The opportunity for deep and meaningful identity is regularly missed in pursuit of buying more gifts or adding more pointless aspects that distract from the core intention of the moment.

It is difficult to single out illustrations of these missed moments as some families have attached depth of meaning to traditions that others might overlook. One practice that seems to intentionally distract from meaning and gratitude in American culture is Black Friday. Traditionally it's the day after Thanksgiving when businesses often move from the red (deficit in spending) to the black (profit) due to the surge in purchasing for Christmas gifts. It is surrounded with advertisements, sales, and Christmas decorations to entice buyers to be generous in their buying. However, Christmas greetings are continually being replaced with Happy Holidays, and each year the sales start earlier and earlier. Then the sales moved to Thanksgiving Day. Families were tempted to devour their turkey, recite quick gratitudes on their way out the door, and go get the best deals of the year. It's difficult to reconcile Thanksgiving and Christmas with this spike in consumerism, yet most families tend to easily allow the culture to dictate their practice of both traditions and replace them with consumerism.

However, even Black Friday can be utilized for a greater good and depth of meaning. My brother and I developed a redemptive focus of this marketing scheme by starting an organization called Black Friday Cause. We camped out by stores and then bought technology for non-profit organizations while inviting others to join us through giving and watching our live stream experience. We intentionally injected meaning and brought our family's value of giving to the forefront. After doing this for several years and sales moving to Thanksgiving Day, we stopped our practice, but we still remember fondly our experiences of generosity and hilarious moments messing with overzealous shoppers and encouraging overwhelmed workers.

I am currently writing this chapter on National Step in a Puddle and Splash Your Friends Day. It's important to recognize that we can't celebrate every festival or national day of whatever or holiday. We need to decide in advance *what* we will celebrate and *how* we will emphasize meaning and value in each tradition we observe. Certain practices need to be lifted to greater positions of importance, while others should decrease or at times be removed altogether. Your family traditions should include markers of family heritage, milestones for individuals, faith-emphasizing celebrations, and family mission renewal opportunities. These range from annual opportunities to mark our current phase of family to birthdays, anniversaries, holidays, vacations, and major milestones such as weddings, rites of passage, graduations, and funerals.

Traditions are meant to look backward to remind and forward to inspire and celebrate in the present to anchor us in a grander narrative. Christian families experience the annual traditions of Christmas and Easter to remind them of Christ's coming to earth as a child, His sacrifice for the salvation of humankind, and His conquering of death through His resurrection. These traditions also inspire families to look forward to Jesus's second coming and His final destruction of the power of death and sin. As families celebrate, their faith is often renewed as they prepare room in their hearts for Christ to dwell and joyfully worship the risen Savior for His completed work. These traditional practices are built into our calendars with expected celebrations, but too often we are easily distracted by elves, bunnies, and consumer characters that prevent us from drinking deeply of these formative opportunities. Without an intentional plan for our family traditions, we will allow our culture to develop a plan for us.

Take time to assess your traditions through these questions:

- What holidays or traditions does our family practice regularly?
- What do members of our family look forward to in each tradition?
- What aspect of each tradition is the most meaningful for faith or identity? If nothing, what could it be?
- What aspect of each tradition distracts us from the opportunity to celebrate well?
- What can we experience prior to each day of celebration to build up or gradually increase expectation or preparation? (Some examples include Advent, Lent, journaling, fasting, etc.)
- What practice can we implement to improve our approach as a family to traditions and celebrations?

Journey

Traditions have the opportunity to serve as "M-A-P-S" for our journey toward fulfilling our family mission. As we look at our annual calendar, we can find opportunities to make the most of each Milestone marker, Anchor for faith, and Phase of life, and then emphasize them with Stones of remembrance. Family life is filled with challenges and hurdles to overcome that repeatedly rob us of joy and connection. Traditions give opportunity to rise above the current chaos to celebrate enduring truth and values that fuel us for the journey through life's challenges. As we rethink these opportunities and plan in advance, we are able to maximize our mission and enjoy building anticipation toward life's greatest moments.

M – Milestones

A milestone is a significant event or stage in life, progress, and development. Major milestones deserve to be celebrated with magnificence and meaning. Significant events for your family deserve an investment of time and money. For example, it is ideal to set aside a separate savings account to prepare well in advance for weddings. A wedding marks the merging of two families and the enduring opportunity to extend your multigenerational team and family mission. Other cultures mark this milestone with a week-long celebration to emphasize its significance and to enable families to relationally merge together. Preparations are often made for months, if not years, in advance to maximize the significance of this major milestone. The wedding ceremony and reception yield tremendous opportunities to emphasize your family mission and inject meaning into common practices. Extraordinary celebration in the major milestone of a wedding can declare the immense value of marriage to all who attend since "marriage should be honored by all" (Heb. 13:4).

Milestones demand attention and commemoration in order to reflect importance. We are regularly so busy with our current expectations that it is easy to lessen the significance of key moments in our lives. Yet when we take time to emphasize milestones, we reward the accomplishment or significance with value. The moments we reward for one will have increased probability to be repeated by others. Simply stated, whatever is rewarded is often repeated.

Everyone has a desire to be celebrated for their contribution and personal accomplishments. When we tie these to the advancement of our family mission, we realize the weightiness of these milestones. A funeral marks the passing of leadership and the celebration of the life of a loved one. Graduations mark academic accomplishment and movement toward the personal ability to carry the family heritage forward. A rite of passage ceremony can develop a depth of identity as a man or woman carries the family name. Bearing a child, achieving a 40th anniversary, buying a first home, launching a business, and retirement are a few examples of milestones families emphasize with significant celebrations.

- What are key milestones on your family's journey?
- How can you emphasize celebrations of significance for each one?

A – Anchors

Western civilization is unquestionably built on a calendar that reflects the Christian faith. Most businesses are closed on Christmas and Christmas Eve, as well as Easter and even Good Friday for some. Throughout Christian history and internationally today in persecuted nations, these holidays have been celebrated without the blessing of or in direct opposition to the surrounding culture. In these circumstances, Christmas stands as a time of increased scrutiny and persecution. Christians gathering in secret house churches to sing and celebrate invariably lead to violent arrests and lengthy imprisonments. Why would they risk imprisonment and death to celebrate a holiday? They would rather die for something than live for nothing. Observing a religious holiday is an anchor of identity. The accompanying signs and symbols deeply root the believer with the greater community and family of faith.

The primary danger in the Western world is not persecution for celebrating but the secularization of these holidays to the point of meaninglessness. In a melting pot of religious and irreligious practices and experiences, holidays tend to devolve into self-centered consumerism. To resist this slide into conformity with culture, Christian families have the opportunity to anchor their faith through sacrificial practice and joyful celebration. "This is how we know what love is: Jesus Christ laid down his life for us. And we ought to lay down our lives for our brothers and sisters" (1 John 3:16).

Jesus demonstrated His overwhelming love and commitment to save those separated from God by sacrificing His life on behalf of others. Through this sacrifice, He modeled the ongoing practice for Christians to be willing to give up now in order to gain greater rewards later. Love for God is best demonstrated in sacrificial love for others in the name of Jesus. Intentionally sacrificing something declares the worthiness of the one for whom it is sacrificed. Jewish festivals almost always involved a sacrifice of some type to declare their commitment to God or to renew their faith in Him as their source of life and provision.

Lent and Advent were designed as gradual increases of teaching and preparation for the great crescendos of Easter and Christmas. Lent specifically involves fasting from something for 40 days until Easter as a reminder of Christ's fasting in the wilderness and His sacrifice on our behalf. Christian fasting is intentionally withholding something we'd normally partake of for the purpose of creating space in our lives to feast on the presence of Jesus. The celebration of freedom on Easter has greater depth of meaning when we have prepared our hearts through intentional sacrifice.

Advent invites Christians to build toward Christmas with intentional teaching and time together as a family. The four Sundays prior to Christmas allow time to anchor the family through teaching and symbolic practice so they can celebrate more fully the meaning of Christmas. Families deepen their faith experience through intentional service and financial investments in God's work as a sacrificial gift to Christ.

Additionally, the celebrations of key anchors of faith should incite anticipation and excitement through annual practices. Joy is contagious as it draws everyone in our family and those we are connected with to see the value we place on these traditions. Life should not reflect business as usual. Signify these traditions with celebratory food, drinks, and practices that reflect depth of meaning and joyful sharing. Our family regularly celebrates with Christmas crepes and resurrection rolls for breakfast and afternoon feasts for lunch and dinner. These celebrations scream, "This matters! This is where life is found! He is worthy!"

P – Phases

There is an old saying that attempts to alleviate the challenges of certain seasons of family life—"It's just a phase; you'll get through it." While it is helpful to have hope that things will not always be this way, there is also the potential to approach every phase with this mindset. Every phase has its own joys and challenges. Families often wish away their current season in pursuit of an easier time that…never…comes. Then parents often dream of the days they previously wished away as the time they long to return to. It's important to embrace the current season as you enjoy the joys and endure the challenges. We should be able to say, "It's just a phase; don't miss it."[16] The time you are in today matters. Make the most of each phase while you have it.

Birthdays are important markers of development. Celebrating birthdays with value and meaning emphasizes the importance of each individual to your multigenerational family team. Develop a practice that rises above simplistic gift-giving to deepen family identity. A couple practices we have regularly employed are word gifts and birthday blessings. Word gifts are usually given by all who gather for the birthday party through words of encouragement and gratitude for the celebrated one. In a culture that significantly lacks encouragement and positive reinforcement, this practice stands out as unique and memorable for all who attend. We usually speak a birthday blessing over the person to begin a new year of growth and impact.

Anniversaries also signify enduring commitment in marriage as a foundation for strong family teams. Each phase of marriage has its own joys and challenges. Dedication to emphasize these annual markers offers opportunity to renew commitment and restore connection. Annually, my wife and I retreat together for at least two nights to raise the importance of our marriage to each other and our children. Many years have posed significant challenges and tested our resolve, but deciding in advance has caused us to do whatever is necessary to make this possible. We keep in mind that generations will benefit from our depth of connection and commitment.

Don't miss the joys of the phase in which you are currently living. "Rejoice always, pray continually, give thanks in all circumstances; for this is God's will for you in Christ Jesus" (1 Thess. 5:16–18). Rejoicing, praying, and giving thanks in whatever season of life you find yourself is literally God's will for your life. While the challenges in each phase are obvious, the joys are easily overlooked. Developing a tradition for the new year, a Thanksgiving ritual, or an annual family summit can give you an opportunity to express gratitude for the past year and set goals and hopes for the year ahead. You will never live this phase of family life again. Don't miss it.

S – Stones

Great moments deserve to be remembered and commemorated. Throughout Scripture we find altars and stones set up as memorials of God's leadership and deliverance. Joshua marked the movement from wandering in the wilderness to possessing the Promised Land with stones of remembrance from the Jordan River.

> [Joshua] told them, "Go into the middle of the Jordan, in front of the Ark of the LORD your God. Each of you must pick up one stone and carry it out on your shoulder—twelve stones in all, one for each of the twelve tribes of Israel. We will use these stones to build a memorial. In the future your children will ask you, 'What do these stones mean?' Then you can tell

them, 'They remind us that the Jordan River stopped flowing when the Ark of the LORD's Covenant went across.' These stones will stand as a memorial among the people of Israel forever."

—Josh. 4:5-7 (NLT)

Samuel raised a massive stone in the middle of the wilderness to remind the Israelites of their victory over the Philistines. "He named it Ebenezer (which means 'the stone of help'), for he said, 'Up to this point the LORD has helped us!'" (1 Sam. 7:12).

In these scenarios, the message was clear—God has done it! We can trust Him to lead us forward. Stones of remembrance serve as a reminder of God's faithfulness in the past and renew our courage in the present. Significant moments on your family journey and in your family mission should be notably sealed as stones of remembrance. Our family's mission statement is displayed artistically in our living room. It serves as a daily reminder and weekly emphasis during our Sabbath meal of our unique calling by God to live out our family mission. In an oversaturated culture of messages and advertisements, a "mission stone" will help everyone know what really matters and serve as a standard of accountability in your home. Historically, a coat of arms reinforced this depth of identity and family heritage.

Stones of remembrance are best utilized for major milestones or to retell significant stories from your family journey. Too often we forget God's faithfulness and His activity in our lives. As our memories fade, our fears and worries of future provision and protection grow. There are certain family stories everyone should be able to tell. Stones of remembrance anchor these moments as cornerstone stories to be revisited regularly. To help guide you to choose memorable reminders for your family, use the following questions:

- What are significant moments that have transformed our family?
- What physical object(s) could we place in our home that would serve as reminders of these experiences?
- How will we commemorate major milestones in our family? What could serve as meaningful markers of these events?
- How could we display our family mission in our home to emphasize its significance?

Celebration

What is a man? What is a woman? These are fundamentally core yet emotionally loaded questions. In a culture that celebrates confusion of gender and sexuality, the next generation needs someone to clarify the character and roles of a godly man and woman. While I do not intend to unpack the answers to these questions here, I do recognize the danger of leaving them unanswered. Your child needs to know with clarity a target of character to aim for. If we do not guide the next generation in pursuit of manhood or womanhood, they will find themselves lost and looking for validation. Their source of validation in our culture usually becomes some avenue of achieving adult status through graduation, a first job, getting married, having sex, moving out, purchasing a car or house, or reaching a specific age. At what age does someone become a man or a woman? 12? 13? 16? 18? 21? 25? 30? While some point to the beginning of a menstrual cycle for a girl as her transition into womanhood, a boy does not have the same clear physical marker. Also, due to the expansion of adolescence and emergence of a longer single adulthood, the next generation grasps for the freedoms of adulthood earlier while dodging its responsibilities as long as possible.

Many cultures have solutions to this adulthood ambiguity through specific ceremonies or ages of accountability. Jewish boys and girls celebrate their Bar and Bat Mitzvahs at ages 13 and 12, respectively, in order to demonstrate their commitment to their faith and age of responsibility to follow Jewish law. Many Hispanic cultures practice a Quinceañera celebration to mark a 15-year-old girl's passage into womanhood. This typically begins with a Catholic mass where the girl renews her baptismal vows and solidifies her commitment to her family and faith. Immediately following the mass is a fiesta where friends and family eat and dance. In Japan, the second Monday of January marks Seijin no Hi, a coming-of-age festival when the Japanese believe youth become mature, contributing members of society and are given the right to vote and drink. Tribal experiences include land diving, cow jumping, or enduring intense pain without flinching. While these practices have endured throughout centuries in varying cultures, the modern American culture possesses no correlating event.

These valuable practices signify an important principle. A boy becomes a man when an older man tells him he is one. A girl becomes a woman when she is affirmed as a woman by an older woman. Manhood and womanhood are not achieved; they are received. Young men and women are craving someone to validate them and tell them they have what it takes. If an older man declares it, that helps settle a boy's soul and striving. Without this declaration, many girls wrestle with their identity and ability to carry their family heritage forward.

Our church recognized this important opportunity to offer a solution for this developmental gap. We developed processes called Passed Thru Fire and Daughters of the King to affirm an early passage into young adulthood. These were father-son and mother-daughter experiences that included eight weeks of teaching and a culminating event. Both included the valuable elements of teaching, affirmation, and sealing. Teaching consisted of a shared reading plan to be discussed first in parent-child relationships and later as a group. There were several aspects of affirmation through letters from influential adults and verbal affirmation in front of the larger group to declare manhood or womanhood by fathers or mothers. Finally, this moment was sealed by some type of stone of remembrance or keepsake to remind them of the experiences they shared together.

These processes usually happened around middle school. Later experiences—Xtreme Weekend and Radiant Sleepover—marked adulthood after graduating from high school. Again, these experiences included teaching, affirmation, and culminating events to signify the transition from young adulthood into mature and contributing members of church and family. There is a wide variety of ceremonies families have chosen to mark this important milestone, from campouts, skydiving, chopping down a tree, and holding a multigenerational feast to passing a baton. The emerging adult will benefit from personal effort, challenges, and overcoming obstacles to develop a greater understanding of opportunity and responsibility as a contributing man or woman.

Some families reading this may not have an expected cultural or communal rite of passage experience. It will require some planning and intentionality to get started, but future generations will be so grateful for your investment in this. Use these questions to guide you as you prepare for a meaningful rite of passage experience.

- What age will we target for this experience for boys and girls?
- Is there a progression of events to build up to the final ceremony?

- What character attributes do we want to emphasize for manhood and womanhood?
- How will we mark the uniqueness of our family heritage in signifying adulthood?
- What skills do we want to pass on to or empower the next generation with?
- Who do we want to have present or give the opportunity to speak affirmation over the next generation?
- What will be the climactic moment to signify the completion of the process or passage into adulthood?
- What gift can we give to serve as a continual reminder of this transition into adulthood?

As you process through a meaningful milestone signifying manhood and womanhood, meditate on the importance of the foundation of God's Word to guide the next generation.

> The heavens proclaim the glory of God.
> The skies display his craftsmanship.
> Day after day they continue to speak;
> night after night they make him known.
> They speak without a sound or word;
> their voice is never heard.
> Yet their message has gone throughout the earth,
> and their words to all the world.
> God has made a home in the heavens for the sun.
> It bursts forth like a radiant bridegroom after his wedding.
> It rejoices like a great athlete eager to run the race.
> The sun rises at one end of the heavens
> and follows its course to the other end.

Nothing can hide from its heat.
The instructions of the LORD are perfect,
   reviving the soul.
The decrees of the LORD are trustworthy,
   making wise the simple.
The commandments of the LORD are right,
   bringing joy to the heart.
The commands of the LORD are clear,
   giving insight for living.
Reverence for the LORD is pure,
   lasting forever.
The laws of the LORD are true;
   each one is fair.
They are more desirable than gold,
   even the finest gold.
They are sweeter than honey,
   even honey dripping from the comb.
They are a warning to your servant,
   a great reward for those who obey them.
How can I know all the sins lurking in my heart?
   Cleanse me from these hidden faults.
Keep your servant from deliberate sins!
   Don't let them control me.
Then I will be free of guilt
   and innocent of great sin.
May the words of my mouth
   and the meditation of my heart
be pleasing to you,
   O LORD, my rock and my redeemer.

—Ps. 19 (NLT)

CHAPTER 7

Future Family

Legacy

*W*HAT IN YOUR current life will still matter 150 years from now? That number—150—is intriguing because there is no way you will live that long. But beginning with a timeline that extends beyond our lifetime reminds us to invest in what lasts. When we keep a long-term timeline in view, it guides us to faithfully contribute to the good of future generations instead of seeking short-term personal gain. Truly there are only two aspects of our lives that will last eternally—God and people. A famous poem by C. T. Studd repeats this refrain: "Only one life, 'twill soon be past, only what's done for Christ will last."[17]

God and His Word will last forever. This realization along with the brokenness of earthly pursuits led King David to his ultimate desire to "dwell in the house of the LORD forever" (Ps. 23:6). Those who receive Christ as Savior and follow Him as Lord are assured of an eternal family and dwelling in an eternal home with God as an ever-present Father. This is an unshakable promise because God has declared it. He has invited humankind to join His eternal, forever family through the sacrifice of His Son on their behalf. This forever family will be perfect and unblemished by sin, comparison, envy, sibling rivalry, arguments around the dinner table, relational tension, disappointments, and pain since "the former things have passed away" (Rev. 21:4 ESV). Time spent pursuing God and building His kingdom in this life are wise investments with eternal returns.

People will also experience eternity either in the Father's presence or separated from Him. God in His infinite wisdom and love has enabled people to join Him forever by receiving His gift of grace. Or people may reject His offer and live for themselves. When we truly pause to recognize every person we interact with as an eternal soul, it changes our view of the moment we share together. Every person matters—forever. These truths should cause a stirring in our hearts that makes us want to run through the streets reminding everyone of God's eternal love. Yet the greatest long-term impact is not simply speaking a message but training disciples. Jesus spent time teaching crowds, but He spent even more time training His closest followers. Sharing the love of God with people is great, but one step further is doing it alongside others who will continue this pattern long after you have passed away. The multiplication of discipleship has a far greater potential outcome than individual addition through doing it all yourself. We all need a multigenerational approach that centers us in the moment we are living in.

One key practice to encourage personal and kingdom growth in discipleship is the four relationships.

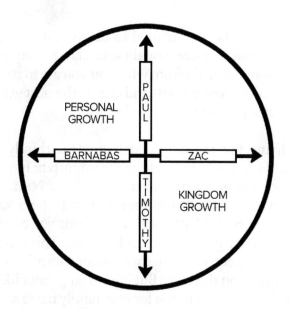

We all need a Paul, Barnabas, Timothy, or Zac in our lives in order to experience maximum growth and impact. A Paul might serve as a mentor to guide you forward with wisdom and insight. A friend and accountability partner who runs the race alongside you is a Barnabas. We also need to be investing in a Timothy, a mentee, to pass on what has been entrusted to us. Finally, our hearts lead us to a Zacchaeus, a type of relationship with someone who doesn't yet know Jesus. These relationships guide, encourage, equip, and enable us to invest our lives in intentional relationships with lasting fruit.

However, when we tried linking people with these relationships, it proved to be difficult based on differing seasons and stages of life. We realized the importance and pressed forward, encouraging and declaring the vital nature of these relationships. Then it became apparent that God had already given many of us these opportunities in our families. We often look around for ministry opportunities and overlook the most important relationships that have already been entrusted to us. As you process these relationships, you may not have these available in your current family, but you can begin from wherever you are to strengthen the opportunities that do exist and enable the next generation to have greater possibilities.

Imagine living out the five fundamentals faithfully for one generation. How could that restore the important foundations of family for the next generation to stand on? Next, imagine gathering with your grandchildren to watch them lead their children through a Sabbath meal and inviting you to speak the final blessing over your great-grandchildren. This is obviously not a guaranteed outcome since we cannot control or force our kids to continue on this path. But it has a far greater likelihood if you faithfully develop honor for your family name and model these enduring heritage-building practices.

"Train up a child in the way he should go; even when he is old he will not depart from it" (Prov. 22:6 ESV). Notice that this is a proverb, not a promise. It was never meant to be understood as an absolute promise but rather as a statement of probability. And that leads us to recognize that people often repeat what they know to a greater degree than what they ultimately desire. This is often great news for intentional families and a dangerous reality for families with destructive patterns. Yet anomalies still exist. Some walk away from the best homes seeking their own short-term satisfaction, and others are rescued from broken families to lead God-honoring lives.

It is not all a hopeless rolling of the dice. Your life and investments in family matter. Don't passively hope to leave a legacy of a strong family; lead a legacy through intentionally implementing these important family fundamentals. As you implement these fundamentals, you will find great value in understanding the stage you are in as a parent or grandparent. Your children need your investment in their lives in different ways during their unique phases of development. We often use the four C's to guide our understanding.

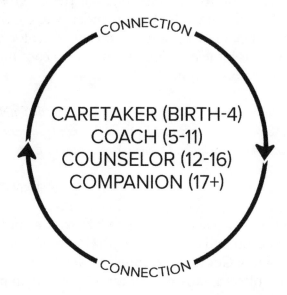

The early years require a lot more hands-on meeting of needs that lead us to physical exhaustion. The older years usually require a higher demand of relational guidance and lead to emotional exhaustion. The overarching goal through all of this, however, is connection throughout each phase, which will build a greater legacy of family identity and lasting relationships. Enjoy the joys of each phase of parenting, and endure the challenges on the path to companionship and connection once they leave your home and carry your family heritage forward. This multigenerational approach brings vision to the necessary sacrifices and invites the next generation not only to be served but to serve and to give their lives to the greater family mission.

Blessing

We have the opportunity with our lives to pass on a curse or a blessing to the next generation. The addictive behaviors present in us often pass on to our offspring, but the generosity and character of Christ in us also have a tendency to continue. As we develop our family team around a mission that glorifies God and casts visions for generations, we pass on a continuance of God's favor and protection.

> *Know therefore that the Lord your God is God; he is the faithful God, keeping his covenant of love to a thousand generations of those who love him and keep his commandments.*

> —Deut. 7:9

This generational blessing is felt in the core of our family identity, direction, and connection with God as one who knows our hearts. Only God has the ability to deliver on a promise like that. He offers a transcendent cause greater than personal desires in the moment to remind us to give up what we want now to gain what we want most. Honoring our family name and heritage is simply worth it. Generations will reap the harvest of our faithfulness to love God and keep His commandments. Sara Groves beautifully sings of this in her song "Generations" as she proclaims peace to her great-great-great-granddaughter.

Your future family begins today as you practice and implement these family fundamentals. As you renew your mind with God's vision for your family and practice Sabbath and meaningful traditions, you will build a solid foundation for future generations. Your great-great-great-grandchildren will experience these blessings and more as you aim your family toward a mission worthy of God's calling and vision. Take time to envision four blessings that could be passed on to your future family.

1. Faith

> *One generation commends your works to another; they tell of your mighty acts.*

—Ps. 145:4

The blessing of a deep and meaningful faith experience is the greatest blessing you can pass on. God's activity in your life is not meant to be privately held in secret but joyfully shared with your family and those you interact with. Our faith expressed with gratitude builds faith in others. Faith is an enduring worldview that anchors us through the trials of life and directs us to the purpose of our existence. Without faith we simply exist without purpose, seeking short-sighted pleasures to satisfy us. As we utilize Sabbath and tradition experiences to consistently build lasting faith, Paul's challenge to the Colossians can become true of our homes.

> *So then, just as you received Christ Jesus as Lord, continue to live your lives in him, rooted and built up in him, strengthened in the faith as you were taught, and overflowing with thankfulness.*

—Col. 2:6-7

We overflow with thankfulness because it is clear in families of faith who every good blessing is from and what it is ultimately for. These blessings come to us to move through us into the lives of others for the glory of the giver of every good gift. We are blessed to be a blessing.

2. Freedom

I love remodeling homes and helping spaces become environments of joy and grace. There is nothing more difficult or usually more expensive in home repair than having to fix the foundation. Many generations inherit cracked foundations from the choices of their parents and grandparents. Our faithfulness today passes on freedom to live and enjoy without the common pitfalls of peer-based identity and building a worldview from scratch.

> You, my brothers and sisters, were called to be free. But do not use your freedom to indulge the flesh; rather, serve one another humbly in love. For the entire law is fulfilled in keeping this one command: "Love your neighbor as yourself."
>
> —Gal. 5:13-14

As we develop a good process that places responsibility before freedom with technology and as we regularly gather to discuss life together around our tables, we can encourage environments of freedom—freedom to love as we desire to be loved, freedom to resist temptation and pursue greater rewards, freedom from the pitfalls of addiction and despair, freedom to truly enjoy now and forever.

3. Financial

> A good person leaves an inheritance to their children's children, but a sinner's wealth is stored up for the righteous.
>
> —Prov. 13:22

It is good to leave an inheritance for our children, but it is even better to pass on the blessing of wisdom on how to manage money. As we embrace the multigenerational team approach to family, we are enabled to work together as stewards of God's resources. An increase in wealth does not always result in an increase in happiness, but teaching the dangers of debt and the joy of generosity will safeguard generations to come. Strong families have a much longer view of finances to invest in long-term returns or develop assets. Generationally connected families have a much higher probability of passing on assets through a long-term stewardship mindset. As an old proverb states, "The best time to plant a tree was 20 years ago. The second best time is now."[18] A stewardship mindset looks more at the lasting fruit of assets than short-term splurges and constant need. It is good to enable stability in your family through a wise financial plan and avoid the frantic nature of living paycheck to paycheck. Your work ethic, generosity, and wise budgeting will model wisdom that will pass on a financial blessing to generations in your family name.

4. Feast

We are invited to an eternal feast of enjoyment and connection. Heaven is not described in Scripture as floating on clouds but metaphorically as a wedding feast. Jesus teaches, "People will come from east and west and north and south, and will take their places at the feast in the kingdom of God" (Luke 13:29).

As you gather for Sabbath dinner to cease working and celebrate the goodness of God each week, you are casting vision for the heavenly feast to come. This extends an invitation to future generations and builds a deep longing for the fullness of time when Jesus will return to restore all things to the way they were originally intended in the Garden of Eden. John writes as it was revealed to him in a vision:

> I saw the Holy City, the new Jerusalem, coming down out of heaven from God, prepared as a bride beautifully dressed for her husband. And I heard a loud voice from the throne saying, "Look! God's dwelling place is now among the people, and he will dwell with them. They will be his people, and God himself will be with them and be their God. 'He will wipe every tear from their eyes. There will be no more death' or mourning or crying or pain, for the old order of things has passed away." He who was seated on the throne said, "I am making everything new!"
>
> —Rev. 21:2–5

Your enjoyment of a family feast is a foretaste of the coming eternal feast that will be experienced without crying, complaining, or chaos. Your heavenly Father invites you to share in a feast of his love and joy forevermore.

Summit

A final practice that will continue to cast vision and guide your family to generational blessing is a Family Summit. This practice should be structured as 90 percent celebration and 10 percent evaluation. Shared experiences and enjoyment of moments together as a multigenerational team will bond you together like an invisible adhesive. The opportunities for this practice are vast. Our family takes a vacation together every other year that is filled with great food, games, and fun. Cousins have the opportunity to deepen relationships, and adults reconnect in unhurried time. We have also made it an annual practice to extend our Thanksgiving break to enjoy more time together with our multigenerational team. Other families celebrate Christmas and New Year's Day together with an opportunity to set goals for the future.

Regardless of the exact timing, it is important to celebrate well together and give opportunity for relational time. Family storytelling has the opportunity to cement your family together as everyone hears stories from different generational experiences. Sitting around a fire pit or at a dining room table with a basic prompt to kick off a conversation can curate encouragement and compassion within your family team. Here are some prompts that usually work well.

- Best Day Ever
- Love Stories
- Trophies
- Troublemaker
- Greatest Games

In the best case scenario, it is honoring to allow the oldest present members of the family to share first and encourage younger generations to listen and ask questions. Spend as much time in this practice as energy and attention spans allow. The value of knowing family stories cannot be understated in developing depth of relationships and ongoing connectedness.

It will also be beneficial for adults and family leaders to spend some time in evaluation. Basic evaluation can involve everyone, but greater intentionality with evaluation demands maturity and the ability to honestly assess. Your family will only have the opportunity to grow in mission and vision as far as you are able to have open evaluation. These questions can enable evaluation and greater intentionality with your future family mission.

- What milestones are we approaching in our family?
- What practices are giving life to our family mission?
- What are avenues for generosity we want to invest in?
- What challenges or transitions will our family face in the coming year?
- How can we invest in the gifts of our children to build generational opportunity?
- What opportunities do we have to meet together and deepen relationships this year?

Your future family begins today as you renew your mind with the Father's wisdom and apply these practices. Continue to do so in an environment of grace for the less than ideal and hope anchored in the foundations of God's enduring truth. "Let us not become weary in doing good, for at the proper time we will reap a harvest if we do not give up" (Gal. 6:9).

As you process these questions and envision your future family, meditate on Proverbs 3.

> *My son, do not forget my teaching,*
> *but keep my commands in your heart,*
> *for they will prolong your life many years*
> *and bring you peace and prosperity.*
> *Let love and faithfulness never leave you;*
> *bind them around your neck,*
> *write them on the tablet of your heart.*
> *Then you will win favor and a good name*
> *in the sight of God and man.*
> *Trust in the LORD with all your heart*
> *and lean not on your own understanding;*
> *in all your ways submit to him,*
> *and he will make your paths straight.*

Do not be wise in your own eyes;
  fear the Lord and shun evil.
This will bring health to your body
  and nourishment to your bones.
Honor the LORD with your wealth,
  with the firstfruits of all your crops;
then your barns will be filled to overflowing,
  and your vats will brim over with new wine.
My son, do not despise the LORD's discipline,
  and do not resent his rebuke,
because the LORD disciplines those he loves,
  as a father the son he delights in.
Blessed are those who find wisdom,
  those who gain understanding,
for she is more profitable than silver
  and yields better returns than gold.
She is more precious than rubies;
  nothing you desire can compare with her.
Long life is in her right hand;
  in her left hand are riches and honor.
Her ways are pleasant ways,
  and all her paths are peace.
She is a tree of life to those who take hold of her;
  those who hold her fast will be blessed.

—Prov. 3:1–18

References

Anderson, Jane E., and Den Trumbull. "The Benefits of the Family Table." *American College of Pediatricians* (February 2021). Accessed February 14, 2021, https://acpeds.org/position-statements/the-benefits-of-the-family-table.

Cloud, Henry, and John Townsend. *How People Grow.* Grand Rapids, MI: Zondervan, 2001.

Comer, John Mark. *The Ruthless Elimination of Hurry.* Colorado Springs: Waterbrook, 2019.

Earley, Justin Whitmel. *The Common Rule.* Downers Grove, IL: InterVarsity Press, 2019.

Fadling, Alan. *An Unhurried Life.* Downers Grove, IL: InterVarsity Press, 2013.

The Social Dilemma. Directed by Jeff Orlowski (2020). *Netflix.*

Joiner, Reggie. *Think Orange.* Colorado Springs, CO: David C Cook, 2009.

Joiner, Reggie, and Kristen Ivy. *Don't Miss It.* Cumming, GA: Orange, 2016.

Klepeis, Neil E., William C. Nelson, Wayne R. Ott, et al. "The National Human Activity Pattern Survey." *Journal of Exposure Science & Environmental Epidemiology, 11,* 231–252 (2001). Accessed January 14, 2021, https://www.nature.com/articles/7500165.

Lewis, C. S. *The Screwtape Letters.* Cheshire, England: Geoffrey Bles, 1942.
Pryor, Jeremy. *Family Revision.* Family Teams, 2019.

Reinke, Tony. *12 Ways Your Phone Is Changing You.* Wheaton, IL: Crossway, 2017.

Wang, Wendy, and Kim Parker. "Record Share of Americans Have Never Married." *Pew Research Center.* September 24, 2014. Accessed February 14, 2021, https://www.pewresearch.org/social-trends/2014/09/24/record-share-of-americans-have-never-married/.

Witt, Lance. *Replenish: Leading from a Healthy Soul.* Grand Rapids, MI: Baker Books, 2011.

Zomorodi, Manoush, Ariana Tobin, and Jen Poyant. "Get a Grip on Your Information Overload with 'Infomagical.'" *NPR.* January 25, 2016. Accessed January 5, 2021, https://www.npr.org/sections/alltechconsidered/2016/01/25/463232382/get-a-grip-on-your-information-overload-with-infomagical.

Endnotes

[1]   "Vince Lombardi Jr. Quotes," *Goodreads*, https://www.goodreads.com/
quotes/219260-football-is-like-life—it-requires-perserverance-self-denial-hard.

[2]   Coach Vincent T. Lombardi, "What It Takes to Be Number One," *Vince Lombardi*,
http://www.vincelombardi.com/number-one.html.

[3]   Wendy Wang, and Kim Parker, "Record Share of Americans Have Never
Married," *Pew Research Center*, September 24, 2014, https://www.pewresearch.org/
social-trends/2014/09/24/record-share-of-americans-have-never-married/.

[4]   C. S. Lewis, *The Screwtape Letters*, Cheshire, England: Geoffrey Bles, 1942.

[5]   "Socrates: Philosopher of the Week," *Kids Philosophy Slam*, http://www.
philosophyslam.org/socrates07.html.

[6]   "Justin Whitmel Earley," *Goodreads*, https://www.goodreads.com/author/
quotes/18324595.Justin_Whitmel_Earley#:~:text=%E2%80%9CHabits%20
form%20much%20more%20than,%3A%20they%20form%20
our%20hearts.%E2%80%9D&text=%E2%80%9CThe%20daily%20
habit%20of%20one,dependent%20and%20communal%20human%20
beings.%E2%80%9D.

[7]   Wayne Muller, quoted in Lance Witt, *Replenish: Leading from a Healthy Soul*,
Grand Rapids, MI: Baker Books, 2011, 128.

8   Jane E. Anderson, and Den Trumbull, "The Benefits of the Family Table," *American College of Pediatricians*, February 2021, https://acpeds.org/position-statements/the-benefits-of-the-family-table.

9   Manoush Zomorodi, Ariana Tobin, and Jen Poyant, "Get a Grip on Your Information Overload with 'Infomagical,'" *NPR*, January 25, 2016, https://www.npr.org/sections/alltechconsidered/2016/01/25/463232382/get-a-grip-on-your-information-overload-with-infomagical.

10   Tony Reinke. *12 Ways Your Phone Is Changing You.* Wheaton, IL: Crossway, 2012.

11   Neil E. Klepeis, William C. Nelson, Wayne R. Ott, et al. "The National Human Activity Pattern Survey (NHAPS): A Resource for Assessing Exposure to Environmental Pollutants." *Journal of Exposure Science & Environmental Epidemiology, 11*, 231–252 (July 26, 2001), https://www.nature.com/articles/7500165.

12   "Children in Nature," *National Recreation and Park Association*, https://www.nrpa.org/uploadedFiles/nrpa.org/Advocacy/Children-in-Nature.pdf.

13   *The Social Dilemma*, directed by Jeff Orlowski (2020), *Netflix*.

14   Ibid.

15   "crescendo," *Merriam-Webster*, https://www.merriam-webster.com/dictionary/crescendo.

16   Reggie Joiner, and Kristen Ivy, *Don't Miss It*, Cumming, GA: Orange, 2016.
17   "Quotes of C.T. Studd," *WebTruth.org*, https://www.webtruth.org/great-quotes/quotes-c-t-studd/

18   "Chinese Proverbs Traditional," *Goodreads*, https://www.goodreads.com/quotes/2704080-the-best-time-to-plant-a-tree-was-20-years.

CPSIA information can be obtained
at www.ICGtesting.com
Printed in the USA
LVHW050218040621
689239LV00014B/1680